EXPERIENCING JESUS THROUGH

COMMUNION

BENI JOHNSON

WITH BILL JOHNSON

EXPERIENCING JESUS THROUGH

COMMUNION

A 40-DAY PRAYER JOURNEY TO UNLOCK THE
DEEPER POWER OF THE LORD'S SUPPER

DESTINY IMAGE® PUBLISHERS, INC.
P.O. Box 310, Shippensburg, PA 17257-0310
"Promoting Inspired Lives."

This book and all other Destiny Image and Destiny Image Fiction books are available at Christian bookstores and distributors worldwide.

Cover design by Eileen Rockwell

For more information on foreign distributors, call 717-532-3040.

Reach us on the Internet: www.destinyimage.com.

ISBN 13 TP: 978-0-7684-5634-9

ISBN 13 eBook: 978-0-7684-5635-6

ISBN 13 HC: 978-0-7684-5636-3

For Worldwide Distribution, Printed in the U.S.A.

1 2 3 4 5 6 7 8 / 25 24 23 22 21

CONTENTS

Day 1:

THE POWER OF COMMUNION

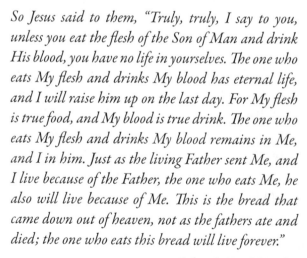

So Jesus said to them, "Truly, truly, I say to you, unless you eat the flesh of the Son of Man and drink His blood, you have no life in yourselves. The one who eats My flesh and drinks My blood has eternal life, and I will raise him up on the last day. For My flesh is true food, and My blood is true drink. The one who eats My flesh and drinks My blood remains in Me, and I in him. Just as the living Father sent Me, and I live because of the Father, the one who eats Me, he also will live because of Me. This is the bread that came down out of heaven, not as the fathers ate and died; the one who eats this bread will live forever."

—John 6:53-58 NASB

I was raised in the church. As the saying goes, "I cut my teeth on the wooden pews." My parents were never officially pastors, but they were always leaders in the church. We called them "lay pastors." They weren't licensed, but they helped in the church, mostly with the youth, and were there all of the time.

We definitely spent a lot of time in those wooden pews. For us, though, being at church was just a normal part of life. I never resented how often we were there. I loved it. I don't remember ever complaining about going to church. That was where our community was; it was how we did family.

I also loved getting to be a part of what God was doing. I suppose that, even then, I was a people-watcher. When the minister would give the altar call, inviting people to come up front and give their lives to the Lord, I would walk right down and sit on the ground by the first pew. I remember one time, the pastor invited people to come to the front to encounter more of the Lord.

I immediately went right down and sat at the end of the first pew. People began to come up, and right away they started to manifest physically. They were crying and rolling around on the ground, encountering the Holy Spirit in new ways. This was many years before the renewal in the '90s, when this kind of activity became a bit more normal. I had no idea what was going on! But I knew it was the Lord. I don't remember being scared at all. Even as child, I loved seeing how encountering God changed people.

Our church, like most churches, had a monthly tradition of taking Communion as a congregation. All those who knew Christ as their Savior celebrated the death and resurrection by sharing in Communion. As a young girl, I thought the best part of this was that I got to eat a little wafer and drink a doll-sized cup of juice. That was pretty fun! At that time, I was getting to participate in the joy and celebration of Communion, but it would be many years before I began to fully experience and understand the power of this tool that Jesus gave us.

Father, I long to encounter You in a tangible way today. As I hold the elements of communion in my hands, help me to be physically, mentally, and spiritually aware of Your presence.

This is Your body, broken for me.

This is Your blood, poured out for me.

Thank You, Jesus, for all that You've done!

A TOOL OF INTERCESSION

Pray passionately in the Spirit, as you constantly intercede with every form of prayer at all times. Pray the blessings of God upon all his believers.

—Ephesians 6:18 TPT

I have always taken Communion whenever I have felt prompted by the Holy Spirit. As an intercessor, I have included Communion as a part of my prayer time. It has always been wonderful and powerful. However, it wasn't until Bill got sick several years ago that I grabbed on to Communion in a more intentional way. Something shifted for me.

Since that time of taking Communion daily in the hospital with Bill, I don't wait for Communion Sunday at church or even for the Lord's nudging. I've started to take Communion as a tool in my intercessory toolbox, as a purposeful and proactive part of my relationship with the Lord. I usually take it every day, sometimes multiple times a day, and this new intentionality has shifted my expectation and understanding of the power behind that little wafer and small cup of juice.

On Sunday, April 9, 2017, our church body ended a corporate fast. My husband preached a wonderful sermon on the impact of Communion, and at the end of the service we took Communion as a congregation. We prayed together, applied the blood of Jesus to our families and communities, and celebrated what Jesus did for all mankind. That morning, I prayed—like I always did—for each of my family members. But I also felt moved to pray for two of my best friends' children who were lost in their spiritual lives. I pleaded the blood of Jesus over their lives and remembered all that Jesus had done for them when He went to the cross. Even after we were finished taking Communion, though, I couldn't shake the feeling that I was supposed to keep praying for them.

Sometimes the Lord invites us into what I like to call seasons of prayer. These are moments in time when something or someone is put on our heart to pray for, and we just can't let it go. In those seasons, the Holy Spirit will press upon us to keep praying for that specific person or issue. This intense focus may last just a day or much longer. And, in that time of prayer, we may get to see the answer to our prayers or we may just be invited into the process without seeing any specific results. But either way, we continue to pray because we are being pulled to do so. And usually, just as quickly as the season of prayer comes, it will lift.

Praying for the children of my friends lasted for several days. At the end of that time, I knew that I was released from that season of prayer when these two individuals were lifted from my heart. Not that I didn't still love and pray for them, but they weren't constantly in front of my face. Even though there hasn't been a conclusion to their story yet—these two are both still on their journey back to the Lord—I know that that time of praying for them intentionally and taking Communion, pleading the blood of Jesus over their lives, was fruitful. In these moments, we may not always be able to see the direct results of our prayers, but we can rest assured that another seed was planted.

Holy Spirit, as I take communion today, bring to mind someone whom You would have me pray for. I want to partner with You to intercede on behalf of my loved ones. Increase my sensitivity to Your voice and Your prompting as I pray.

I take Your body, resting in the assurance that You are the bread of life for every single person.

I take Your blood, pleading Your blood over the lives and hearts of those individuals You brought to mind.

Father, I trust that You are working Your plan for redemption in every person You brought to mind. I say "yes" and "amen" to everything You are doing on the earth.

Day 3:

JOY-FILLED PRAYER

Rejoice in the Lord always. I will say it again: Rejoice! Let your gentleness be evident to all. The Lord is near. Do not be anxious about anything, but in every situation, by prayer and petition, with thanksgiving, present your requests to God.

—Philippians 4:4-6 NIV

Any time we are entering a season of prayer for an individual or an issue, we are co-laboring with God. When I use Communion during these seasons of prayer, I joyfully get to do my part in declaring Heaven over their lives. One thing that is important for me to watch out for, though, is allowing a spirit of heaviness to remain on me after I pray. Sometimes, when

we get burdened in prayer for someone, the weight of their situation can start to drag us down. I lived this way for many years. Now, I'm really careful about feelings of heaviness. For me, if I start to accept a feeling of heaviness, it will try to take me down a path that leads into depression. I try really hard not to carry it.

At the end of every prayer, I make sure that I surrender that person or situation back to the Lord so I'm not carrying it. I will take Communion, plead the blood of Jesus over that person, and then I have to let it go. It's not healthy for me, and when we carry that heaviness there's also an element of withholding our trust from God. My friends' kids are not aided by my depression. I care deeply about their welfare, but ultimately He's got them. I just get to be on the winning team.

Judy Franklin has worked for Bill and me for over 20 years. Around ten years ago, she heard a teaching on Communion and felt burdened to pray for her son's salvation. When he was six years old, he had accepted Jesus into his heart, and he had been filled by the Holy Spirit as a young man. But as an adult, he had fallen away from the Lord. Judy prayed for him constantly. He was taking drugs and also transporting them across the border of Mexico. He was in such bad shape that she felt like he was near death.

Judy began to take Communion and declare over her son. She started saying things like, "Jesus, You died for Danny. I'm calling on the power of Your blood to bring him back to You. You sacrificed Your body for my son, and because of that I call him back from the powers of darkness." Every morning she did this, not knowing if anything was changing.

But after about six weeks, he came to her, curious about what made her so happy. She told him that her relationship with God was what gave her joy. "I then prophesied who he was in Christ," she said. That Sunday, he joined her at church and went forward for prayer at the end. As he was receiving prayer, he was overcome with the power of Jesus and fell over, receiving immediate deliverance. He stood up a new man, filled with Jesus and free from addiction.

Scripture says that each time we take Communion, we are *"proclaim*[ing] *the Lord's death until He comes"* (1 Cor. 11:26 NASB). When we take the body and blood of Christ, we are reminding ourselves whose we are and what He did for all of us. The commentary in the *Spirit-Filled Life Bible* puts it this way: "Each occasion of partaking is an opportunity to say, proclaim, and confess again, 'I herewith lay hold of all the benefits of Jesus Christ's full redemption for my life—forgiveness, wholeness, strength, health, sufficiency.'" When we use Communion as a tool for intercession, we are not only realigning ourselves with Christ, but we are also proclaiming the reality of Heaven over every area of our lives.

Jesus, thank You that You paid for it all at the cross. There is no burden of heaviness or worry that I have to carry on my own. You have an answer for every single problem I face.

I take Your body today with gratitude, confessing that You sacrificed Yourself so that I might be made whole.

I take Your blood, proclaiming that I am a citizen of Heaven and anticipating breakthrough in every area of my life.

Thank You that I can joyfully access everything that You paid for on the cross. Nothing separates me from the love, protection, and provision of God.

Day 4:

A PROPHETIC ACT

"For I know the plans I have for you," says the Lord. "They are plans for good and not for disaster, to give you a future and a hope. In those days when you pray, I will listen. If you look for me wholeheartedly, you will find me."

—Jeremiah 29:11-13 NLT

When I take Communion, I take it as a prophetic act, applying it to any situation that is weighing on my heart. A prophetic act is a Holy Spirit-inspired physical action that disrupts the atmosphere. Sometimes, I'll feel as though God wants me to do something tangible to activate something that I'm praying into. During those moments, I simply ask the Holy Spirit, "What should I do about this?" Then, I'll feel prompted to, for example, take my shofar into

the prayer house that we have at Bethel or go to a specific place to take Communion. In completing the prophetic act, we are releasing something into the atmosphere that helps the answer to our prayer to break through.

In Exodus, God had the Israelites kill a lamb and put the blood over their doors, signaling to the Spirit of God to pass by without harming the family inside. Moses instructed the Israelites:

> *You shall take a bunch of hyssop and dip it in the blood which is in the basin, and apply some of the blood that is in the basin to the lintel and the two doorposts; and none of you shall go outside the door of his house until morning* (Exodus 12:22 NASB).

The physical lamb's blood didn't save them; the will of God saved them. But the families that participated in this prophetic act were revealing a heart submitted to God. The lamb's blood was a prophetic act that each family did in order to align themselves with God's will and alert the spirit realm as to whom they belonged.

When Jesus led the disciples through Communion, during their Passover meal together, He was creating and modeling a prophetic act that believers could continue implementing. He was giving us a way to align ourselves with Heaven and bring Heaven's reality to earth. Often when I take Communion, I prophesy to myself.

There is something powerful in the spirit realm about the declaration of truth, so I talk to myself out loud. I remind myself who I am—that I'm a daughter of the King and that I'm strong in Him. I pull on the promises of the Bible as they come to mind. I'll say, "I am crucified with Christ" (see Gal. 2:20). I let the reality of the New Covenant wash over me, changing any mindset within me that needs to be changed. I declare over myself, "I have the peace that passes understanding" (see Phil. 4:7). I remind myself that I can walk in His peace no matter what circumstances surround me.

Holy Spirit, I offer up to You that which is weighing heavily on my heart today. What physical action would You have me do as a way to prophesy breakthrough over my own life?

I take communion today as a prophetic act, declaring Your freedom and supernatural intervention over my life.

I take Your body, commanding everything in my body to line up with Heaven.

I take Your blood, celebrating that no area of my life needs to be in darkness today.

Breakthrough is at hand! I am a new creation; I am Your greatly loved child.

Day 5:

A WEAPON OF WARFARE

For it pleased the Father for all the fullness [of deity—the sum total of His essence, all His perfection, powers, and attributes] to dwell [permanently] in Him (the Son), and through [the intervention of] the Son to reconcile all things to Himself, making peace [with believers] through the blood of His cross; through Him, [I say,] whether things on earth or things in heaven. And although you were at one time estranged and alienated and hostile-minded [toward Him], participating in evil things, yet Christ has now reconciled you [to God] in His physical body through

death, in order to present you before the Father holy and blameless and beyond reproach.

—Colossians 1:19-22 AMP

We are at war. We never want to concentrate on anything the devil is doing. We know he's already been defeated! But there is a war constantly going on all around us. We never need to be distracted by the activity of the enemy. But we can be aware of the battle that is going on all around us for our minds, for our authority, for our health, and for our peace. We have the winning hand every time! Every time we take Communion, we remind ourselves that the devil has been defeated. The cross had the final word.

I think everyone has experienced being attacked. I have dealt with health issues, and there are moments when I've been slammed spiritually. I have had to really lay hold of God's promises of peace. I've always considered myself a peaceful person, but I have had to honestly ask myself, *Do I really believe that I can walk in peace when there are so many things attacking that very thing?*

When I'm taking the bread and the wine in a moment like that, I am in a spiritual battle for my health—spirit, soul, and body. Especially when there's something going on in my world that is threatening my wholeness, it's important for me to take Communion more than once a month. It allows me to continually remind myself who I am, who Jesus is, and what He did. Through Communion, I am brought back to the realization of reality—His world is my true reality, not this one.

There's an old hymn I remember singing as a girl, and the words still ring true. "*There is power, power, wonder-working power in the blood of the Lamb. There is power, power, wonder-working power in the precious blood of the Lamb.*" There is enough power in His blood to cancel any curse, to save us from our sins, and to heal our bodies. And that power has not waned in 2,000 years; it is very much alive and well.

Thank You, Father, that I can walk in victory. I am not a victim to any of the schemes of the enemy; I am covered by the resurrection power of Jesus who sits on the throne at the right hand of the Father.

I take Your body, Jesus, claiming absolute protection and strength over my physical body.

I take Your blood, declaring peace and wholeness over every area of my life.

The devil has been defeated; all authority has been stripped from him and returned to Jesus. I live from a place of triumph with Christ.

Day 6:

LIFE IS IN THE BLOOD

For the life of the flesh is in the blood, and I have given it to you upon the altar to make atonement for your souls; for it is the blood that makes atonement for the soul.

—Leviticus 17:11 NKJV

Communion is the reminder that Jesus Himself gave to us the ultimate covenant. It is the body and the blood of Jesus, shed for us. Blue Letter Bible tells us that the Hebrew word for covenant, *beriyth*, is rooted in a word that means "to cut" or "to eat."

Within the expression "cutting a covenant" itself is the graphic depiction of how a covenant was made. When two individuals were cutting a covenant, the ritual included taking a sacrificial animal and dividing the animal into pieces. The two parties would then walk through the scattered carcass, swearing an oath of allegiance in the midst of a path of blood. Essentially, the two parties were making a public declaration that it would be preferable to be like the dismembered animal beneath their feet than to break this promise.

Each blood covenant was a promise of connection, protection, and provision. Like a marriage covenant, where two people are joined into one, the blood covenant created a bond that superseded all other realities. And this was done through the shedding of blood, a public expression that involved the most intimate aspect of life—the blood flowing through our veins.

Blood carries and sustains life. Each blood covenant offered a promise that would enhance life, but it came with the potential cost of life. Unless you're dealing with health issues or you get injured, your blood is probably not something you think of very often. But our blood is miraculous in all that it accomplishes for our bodies. It truly is the river of life. Blood has three main functions: to provide life, health, and protection. The red blood cells transport oxygen from the lungs to every area of the body. They also disperse nutrients and vitamins to the exact parts of the body where they are needed. Our body's very own Amazon Prime!

The white blood cells, along with lymphocytes, help to build the body's entire immune system. Each cell within the blood has a job to do, helping the body to strengthen itself and fight foreign invaders that could make us sick. Some cells build up the immune system; others help the immune system to know exactly what invaders to target. There are certain cells that remember an invasive organism so that the immune system can respond quicker the next time it encounters that same organism. There are other cells that keep the immune system under control so that it doesn't start attacking the good cells within our bodies. What a glorious army the Lord created within us, sustaining and protecting our bodies with this complex combination of blood cells!

When we get a chance to study the intricate way our bodies were created, it gives insight into our walk with the Lord. He is so intentional. It's no accident that blood plays such an integral role in the Bible. There is life in the blood. It's not just a catchphrase.

*God, thank You for the amazing ways You
knit me together. Thank You that You created
me for abundant life in every single
cell of my body.*

*I take Your body that was bruised and
battered so that our bond would
never again be broken.*

*I take Your blood, Jesus, acknowledging that
You spilled Your blood to cut a covenant with
us of connection, protection, and provision.*

*You gave Your life so that we could truly live,
and I will be forever grateful!*

Day 7:

BLOOD COVENANT

Now as they were eating Jesus took bread, and after blessing it, He broke it and gave it to the disciples, and said, "Take, eat; this is My body." And when He had taken a cup and given thanks, He gave it to them, saying, "Drink from it, all of you; for this is My blood of the [new and better] covenant, which [ratifies the agreement and] is being poured out for many [as a substitutionary atonement] for the forgiveness of sins.

—Matthew 26:26-28 AMP

Throughout history, even in cultures that did not know Jesus, the importance of the blood has been paramount. In the ancient world, a promise that

included blood was distinguished as a covenant; it was unlike any other promise you could make. Merriam-Webster defines *covenant* as "a usually formal, solemn, and binding agreement; a written agreement or promise usually under seal between two or more parties especially for the performance of some action." Blood was a crucial part of this contract. By shedding blood, the covenant was an intimate profession of a lifelong promise.

In H. Clay Trumbull's fascinating book, *The Blood Covenant*, he details biblical covenants, but he also examines the tradition throughout the world. One example he finds is that of the Karen people in Burma. The Karens had three levels of truce-making between tribes in that region. The first, and weakest, was eating a meal together, which simply signified that there would be peace for the moment. If the tribes wanted to symbolize a stronger truce, they would plant a tree together. With this truce, peace would exist between the two tribes as long as the tree remained alive. But it was the third kind—the blood covenant—where the true power of the promise was found.

This covenant was of the utmost force. It covered not merely an agreement of peace or truce, but also a promise of mutual assistance in peace and in war. It conveyed to the covenanting parties mutual tribal rights. Made between chiefs, the covenant embraced their entire tribes. If made between individuals, the immediate family and direct descendants of each person were included in the agreement. Life is found in the blood, and by mixing their blood together, the individuals were effectively merging their lives together.

There is an old sheep-farming tradition called lamb grafting. If the ewe (mother sheep) loses her baby to sickness or another tragedy, she will refuse another orphaned lamb, despite her plaintive cries after her lamb's death. Her baby has a specific scent, and she will reject any baby that's not her own. The farmer, however, can take the skin of her dead baby lamb and drape it over the back of the hungry orphan, covering his old smell with the familiar scent. The ewe, thinking that she is smelling her own baby, will accept the orphaned lamb and the baby will survive. Covenants are a covering for those involved. And no one has made greater covenants with His people throughout history than our God.

Your sacrifice on the cross, Jesus, grafted me into the family of God forever. I am one of God's children—with all of the authority and identity that that brings—because of Your death and resurrection.

I take Your body that was broken so that I could be claimed as a co-heir with You.

I take Your blood, knowing that it covers me, merging my life into Yours.

I am no longer on my own. My life is no longer in opposition to God's purpose but directly in line with His vision, protection, and empowerment.

Day 8:

OUR FAITHFUL FATHER

God is not man, that he should lie, or a son of man, that he should change his mind. Has he said, and will he not do it? Or has he spoken, and will he not fulfill it?

—Numbers 23:19 ESV

bram was a wealthy man, but he had no son. What he did have, though, was a wonderful relationship with God. God had spoken throughout Abram's life, and Abram had listened. He had left the land of his family, on God's promise, and had even split away from his nephew, Lot. In a time period when your tribe was your strength and security, Abram's willingness to separate himself and trust the Lord speaks volumes about his relationship with God.

Each time Abram had an encounter with God and was given a promise, he built an altar, a place of remembrance. Abram grew to be an old man, and he had been hearing promises about his descendants for years. But Sarai was still barren.

Abram said, "O Lord God, what will You give me, since I am childless, and the heir of my house is Eliezer of Damascus?" And Abram said, "Since You have given no offspring to me, one born in my house is my heir" (Genesis 15:2-3 NASB95).

I can imagine him thinking to himself, *Okay, I've had all of these promises about the land my future generations are going to inhabit and how my descendants will number like the sand, but I don't even have one child! Has God been talking about my legacy being left to some distant relative this whole time?* But God knew what his heart was asking.

Then behold, the word of the Lord came to him, saying, "This man will not be your heir; but one who will come from your own body shall be your heir." And He took him outside and said, "Now look toward the heavens and count the stars, if you are able to count them." And He said to him, "So shall your descendants be." Then he believed in the Lord; and He credited it to him as righteousness (Genesis 15:4-6 NASB).

This is the kindness of the Lord. Abram needed reassurance on a promise from God that he had held close to his heart. God didn't turn His back on Abram or rebuke him for not having more faith. Instead, God just spoke to him. And, when Abram believed again, God gave Abram points for righteousness!

Thank You, Father, that You are not offended by my need for reassurance. Thank You that every promise You have made over my life will come to pass, because You are faithful.

I take Your body, Jesus, that was sacrificed so that I would have access to every promise of God.

I plead the blood of Jesus over every single promise in my life that is waiting for fulfillment. I declare that You are the Promise-Keeper, faithful to Your word. I take Your blood in remembrance of all that You've done.

I trust Your promises, Lord, more than my current circumstances. I trust You completely!

Day 9:

GOD'S COVENANT PROMISE

He will cover you with His pinions, and under His wings you may take refuge; His faithfulness is a shield and wall.

—Psalm 91:4 NASB

After that, Abram pushed for even more reassurance: "*He said, 'O Lord God, how may I know that I will possess it?'*" (Gen. 15:8 NASB95). He'd just gotten points for believing God, but Abram needed a little more assurance. In response, God cut a covenant with Abram. He tells him about the future of his descendants—how they would be enslaved, but that they would return to inhabit the land. He instructs Abram to bring the animal sacrifice and cut it up.

I love this about the Lord, that He so humbly inhabits human culture. His goal is always connection. There were so many ways He could have handled Abram's insecurity and even so many ways that He could have reiterated the promise, but God chose to cut a covenant with His friend, Abram, in a way that would speak to Abram's heart.

It's clear that Abram was familiar with blood covenants—in just the previous chapter, he had been warned about his nephew's kidnapping by a few men whom the Bible describes as allies of Abram (see Gen. 14:13). These men had cut a covenant with Abram, so they were under obligation to protect him and his family by reporting the abduction. Abram understood covenants. So I imagine that when God suggested making a covenant with him, it would have felt very meaningful.

When it came time to walk through the cut sacrifice, though, only God passed through. "*It came about, when the sun had set, that it was very dark, and behold, a smoking oven and a flaming torch appeared which passed between these pieces*" (Gen. 15:17 NASB). Normally, both parties involved in the covenant would walk through, but this was a God-initiated promise to Abram. God passed through on His own, putting the weight of the covenant behind His words. Abram would have a child, he would leave a legacy, and God would care for his descendants.

Whether they accessed the fullness of His blessing—by following God's way or not—was their choice, but His part of the promise would stand. Soon after this covenant was cut, Isaac was born, and God changed Abram's name to Abraham.

Thank You, Jesus, that You pursued Your creation even to the point of taking on human form. Your choice to come to earth in the form of a baby reveals an astounding humility. Your decision to follow the Father's plan and go to the cross on our behalf is unfathomable.

This is Your body. You endured torture and pain so that I could access freedom and health.

This is Your blood that was cruelly spilled so that Your promise of eternal life and salvation would be available to every person.

I will not let the power of Your covenant go to waste; I want to access everything You died to give me, Jesus.

OUR INHERITANCE

So then let no one boast in men. For all things belong to you, whether Paul or Apollos or Cephas or the world or life or death or things present or things to come; all things belong to you, and you belong to Christ; and Christ belongs to God.

—1 Corinthians 3:21-23 NASB95

Jesus Christ shed His blood to cut a New Covenant with His creation. To forever bridge the divide of sin that had put a chasm between man and God, He initiated a New Covenant that was prophesied by Jeremiah.

"Behold, days are coming," declares the Lord, "when I will make a new covenant with the house of Israel

and the house of Judah...I will put My law within them and write it on their heart; and I will be their God, and they shall be My people" (Jeremiah 31:31-33 NASB).

This New Covenant at once echoed and fulfilled the promises made to Abram. Instead of coming to earth as smoke and fire, God sent His Son to come to earth in human flesh to walk with us. Instead of a sacrificial animal, torn into two to signify the covenant, God offered His own Son—the spotless Lamb—whose body would be broken as the greatest sacrifice.

We are Abraham's promise fulfilled. Scripture says that, through our faith, we have become Abraham's descendants—as numerous as the stars in the sky and blessed by the Lord. *"And if you belong to Christ [are in Him Who is Abraham's Seed], then you are Abraham's offspring and [spiritual] heirs according to promise"* (Gal. 3:29 AMPC). We are *"heirs according to promise."* We are the ones God was telling him about thousands of years ago, the ones who would inherit the promises and blessings of the Lord. We are the ones for whom God is a shield and a great rewarder (see Gen. 15:1).

The Lord changed Abram's name to Abraham, the father of a multitude, but He also changed our names:

No longer do I call you slaves, for the slave does not know what his master is doing; but I have called you friends, for all things that I have heard from My Father I have made known to you (John 15:15 NASB95).

We have access to God in a way that Abraham, the man who was called the friend of God, had only dreamed about. After Jesus' blood was spilled for the New Covenant, we became not only heirs of Abraham, but also co-heirs with Christ. We share in the inheritance of Jesus.

What Jesus did for all of mankind on the cross was unconditional. He will never go back or change His mind. Accessing the fullness of the blessing of this covenant, though, is our choice entirely.

When we take Communion, we are reminding ourselves of His sacrifice and the personal, unprecedented ways this New Covenant affects every area of our lives. *"He took the cup after they had eaten, saying, 'This cup which is poured out for you is the new covenant in My blood"* (Luke 22:20 NASB95). The blood that was shed was a covenant promise for all of eternity.

Nothing would be the same. The blood of Jesus paid for everything. It washed us white as snow so we could enter the presence of the Lord without an intermediary and without fear. The blood of Jesus gave us freedom and authority. Hell has been defeated for all eternity. And now we get to boldly release Heaven on earth.

Holy Spirit, remind me of my new identity in Christ whenever I forget. Whenever I am acting out of fear or lack, bring to mind the covenant that was made on my behalf.

I take Your body, aligning myself with the covenant that was made by Your death and resurrection.

I take Your blood, devoting myself to the pursuit of my full inheritance in You, Jesus.

God has given Himself to me as an inheritance, and I will spend eternity living from that reality toward all of those on earth who are hungry to know our good, good Father.

Day 11:

THE VICTORIOUS BLOOD OF JESUS

The Lord is my shepherd, I lack nothing. He makes me lie down in green pastures, he leads me beside quiet waters, he refreshes my soul. He guides me along the right paths for his name's sake. Even though I walk through the darkest valley, I will fear no evil, for you are with me; your rod and your staff, they comfort me. You prepare a table before me in the presence of my enemies. You anoint my head with oil; my cup overflows. Surely your goodness and love will follow me all the days of my life, and I will dwell in the house of the Lord forever.

—Psalm 23 NIV

Once, I went out to my son's property to walk and take Communion. They live out on 15 acres, so it's a peaceful place to think and pray. While I was meditating on Communion and all that Jesus went through on the cross, a thought popped into my head: "Every time you take Communion, you remind the devil of his failure." There is power in the victorious blood of Jesus.

That power was not just for the salvation of our souls at Calvary; that power is for right now. Romans says that *"the Spirit of life in Christ Jesus has set you free from the law of sin and of death"* (Rom. 8:2 NASB). The blood of Jesus wiped out the power of sin and the judgment that leads to death. Forever. God took back dominion over the earth and kicked out everything that was once ruled by darkness. As heirs with Christ, we have that same authority through Jesus. And when I take Communion, I am not only aligning myself back up with my true identity as a daughter of God, I am also reminding the devil that he lost. The devil has to watch as I celebrate the resurrection power of Jesus.

The New Covenant has been cut, once and forever. Never again would we have to slice a cow on a hill to walk through it as a sacrifice. Never again would the priest have to go into the Holy of Holies, not sure if he would come out alive, in order to rectify the sins of the people for another year. There was a shift in the atmosphere with the death and resurrection of Jesus Christ. It changed everything forever. We take His blood, represented in the wine, as a beautiful memorial of what Jesus did. By His blood, we can be saved, healed, and delivered.

I hold up the body and blood of Jesus in the face of every area of darkness that has tried to impact my life. Devil, you have lost!

I take the body of Christ, announcing the authority I now have through Him to bring Heaven to earth in every area of my life.

I take the blood of Christ, remembering His sacrifice through which I am saved, healed, and delivered.

Thank You, Jesus, that when You said it was finished, You meant that all of eternity had been reclaimed for the Kingdom of God.

Day 12:

HIS BODY, BROKEN FOR US

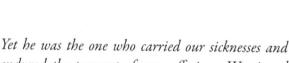

Yet he was the one who carried our sicknesses and endured the torment of our sufferings. We viewed him as one who was being punished for something he himself had done, as one who was struck down by God and brought low. But it was because of our rebellious deeds that he was pierced and because of our sins that he was crushed. He endured the punishment that made us completely whole, and in his wounding we found our healing.

—Isaiah 53:4-5 TPT

In 2015, Bill started getting sick. For months, he had trouble eating and keeping food down. He would have a bad spell, and then his symptoms would seem to disappear for a little while. But then he'd get sick again. He tried changing his diet and getting medical advice, but it wasn't getting better. Finally, in the spring of 2016, while he was teaching in Europe, he became very ill. After speaking one evening, he went back to his hotel room and threw up 20 times. He was able to fly home and, once he got back, we knew we needed some serious help.

We went to our local doctors in Redding, but they said, "We're not touching this one." They sent us to a specialist in San Francisco instead. By this time, Bill wasn't able to eat or drink anything. The hospital put him on an IV to keep him hydrated, and they ran a barrage of tests. Finally, they discovered that there was a growth in his small intestine that was almost completely blocking the passageway. His body was filling up with fluid. The medical staff prepared for surgery to remove the growth, not knowing how invasive of a procedure they would have to do.

Before we went down to San Francisco, before we knew there was a growth, we had begun to take Communion every day at home. We would take the elements, give thanks, and proclaim all that Jesus did on the cross. We would remind ourselves and the enemy that divine health is our birthright. We would declare, "This is Your body, broken for us. This is Your blood that was poured out for us. You died for our sins as well as our sicknesses. We align ourselves—spirit, soul, and body— with all that You did." Bill felt sick, but we were fighting it. And our weapon was Communion.

Once he was in the hospital in San Francisco, he wasn't able to take Communion anymore. He couldn't eat or drink anything at that point. That's when it became serious. We had to beat this thing. Sickness was not going to win. So we said, "The circumstances don't matter; this hospital bed doesn't change a thing. We believe that God is our healer, and we're aligning ourselves with that every single day." So I began to take Communion for him. We would pray together. I would take the elements for myself and for Bill. It was an incredibly sweet time of God's presence. We had so much peace through the whole journey.

As the surgery day drew near, the doctors told us that, unless the mass moved one centimeter away from where it was positioned, they would need to perform a very serious, life-altering procedure. Hearing that, I immediately got the word out to family, friends, and intercessors, asking them to pray and take Communion for this shift. We needed that growth to move! The day of the procedure came and the whole family waited, praying, to hear the news. When the surgeons were done, they gave us the update—the growth had shifted just enough. They were able to perform a procedure that was much less invasive with a quicker healing time. What could have been a scary day became a day of celebration. The whole family was cheering when we got that news. We knew that God had done a miracle.

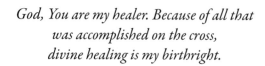

*God, You are my healer. Because of all that
was accomplished on the cross,
divine healing is my birthright.*

This is Your body, broken for me.

This is Your blood, poured out for me.

*You died for my sins as well as my sicknesses.
By taking the elements, I align myself—
spirit, soul, and body—with all that
You did for me.*

Day 13:

FREE FROM SIN, SICKNESS, AND SORROW

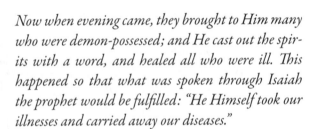

Now when evening came, they brought to Him many who were demon-possessed; and He cast out the spirits with a word, and healed all who were ill. This happened so that what was spoken through Isaiah the prophet would be fulfilled: "He Himself took our illnesses and carried away our diseases."

—Matthew 8:16-17 NASB

J esus died for our sins and for our sicknesses—anything that threatens to steal, kill, or destroy our life in Him is not of Him. When He went to the cross, He carried with Him every dark thing of the enemy and was the eternal sacrifice on our behalf. Isaiah 53:4-5 says:

Surely He has borne our griefs and carried our sorrows; yet we esteemed Him stricken, smitten by God, and afflicted. But He was wounded for our transgressions, He was bruised for our iniquities; the chastisement for our peace was upon Him, and by His stripes we are healed (NKJV).

This passage of Scripture prophesies the crucifixion and the only moment that God had to turn His face from Jesus. When Jesus took the weight of sin upon Himself, there was no way for God to be a part of that. Can you imagine the sorrow that Christ would have experienced? He had known what it was like to live in total union with the Father. I imagine that it would have been crushing for Him to be without God's presence.

Isaiah 53:3, directly prior to the passage above, describes Jesus' rejection by humanity, saying that He was "*A Man of sorrows and acquainted with grief.*" That word *grief* is the Hebrew word *choliy*, meaning sickness, disease, or sadness. It comes from a root word that literally means "to be worn down." Jesus carried all of our sorrows, our anxieties, our illnesses to the cross and died. He took the *choliy* of the world onto His shoulders so that we could be *sozo*—healed in spirit, soul, and body.

When Bill and I were in the hospital taking Communion together in remembrance of all that Jesus had done, healing was a part of that. We knew that healing was ours because of the cross, and we applied it through Communion. I know that there are some who believe that God no longer heals, that all miracles ended with the apostles. This is such a sad thought to me. Jesus endured the unimaginable on the cross in order that we could access salvation and wholeness. We deny the power of the cross when we deny the power of God healing today.

I remember while traveling, years ago, Bill and I were in a coffee shop having something to drink. We noticed a gentleman sitting at the table next to us. He had his Bible open with paper and handwritten notes scattered all around him. He looked like he was in deep study mode. We struck up a conversation with him and very quickly discovered that he was a cessationist. He did not believe that speaking in tongues, prophecy, or healing were for today. We had an interesting discussion with him, and I walked away from that experience with one thought— no one can deny your testimony. When I started sharing what God had done in my life, the gentleman didn't have anything to say. People can argue with theology, but your testimony is your most powerful tool.

When we take Communion, remembering what Jesus accomplished on the cross, we are repeating the ultimate testimony again and again. Jesus Christ died so that we could be free of sin, sickness, and sorrow. He is the healer, and He wants to do it again. Today. Communion has been underutilized far too often. It is a powerful tool, not only for intercession, but also for healing. Take Communion, take it often, and apply the healing power of Jesus to your bodies!

I take authority, today, over anything that has entered my life with the intention of stealing, killing, or destroying. I am a child of God; I live in His blessing. Nothing can take from me what God has given to me as my inheritance in Him.

I take Your body, Jesus, in remembrance of all that You sacrificed so that I might have access to Your complete redemption and Your healing power.

I plead the blood of Jesus over every area of sickness, disease, or sadness in my life.

I step into the fullness of Your sozo healing today!

Day 14:

GOD IS OUR HEALER

*And the prayer of faith will heal the sick and the
Lord will raise them up, and if they have committed
sins they will be forgiven.*

—James 5:15 TPT

Every Saturday morning, we host the Healing
Rooms at Bethel. People come for prayer for all
sorts of physical, emotional, or spiritual ailments.
The first place they go, after they arrive, is into our large
sanctuary that is transformed into an encounter room.
There they can worship, sit quietly, or walk around while
intercessory dancers, artists, and musicians fill the atmosphere with hope and expectancy. There is such a sweet
presence of God there.

Because they know the healing power of Communion, the team leading this encounter room offers our guests the opportunity to take the elements. One woman, who drove up from San Diego, was receiving prayer and taking Communion. She hadn't been able to smell anything for seven years. But while she was lifting the cup to her mouth to drink, suddenly she smelled the juice in the Communion cup. She described feeling as if something had been lifted from her nose!

When we take Communion and declare total health over our bodies, we are aligning ourselves with what the body of Christ did for us. If we believe what the Bible says, that "*by His stripes we are healed*" (Isa. 53:5 NKJV), then there has to be something important in the act of partaking in His body during Communion. His body suffered so that our bodies wouldn't have to. When we take the bread, we are testifying that He is the healer, that we don't have to walk in sickness, that what Jesus did on the cross changed everything.

Elizabeth Lawson, a member of our Bethel community, had dealt with a seizure disorder for 30 years that kept her on a daily regimen of medication. The medication controlled the seizures, so to test out her healing, she would have to take herself off of the pills. She had attempted this many times in the past, working with her doctors to try to taper down the medication in order to see if she was healed. Within three days of weaning off of the medication, she would experience a very intense grand mal seizure. After 30 years of experiencing this, she explained that she had simply resigned herself to being on medication.

However, in the spring of 2013, she began to experience a renewed hope in supernatural healing. One of her friends suggested that she begin taking Communion, using her medication, declaring healing over her body. Following this suggestion, she began to take Communion every night, using her medication and water. She would take the pills in her hand and, out loud, thank Jesus for His death on the cross for her. She would say, "I eat Your body, Lord." Then, taking the glass of water in her hand, she would say, "And I drink Your blood, Jesus."

Elizabeth loved her daily moment of connecting with the Lord over Communion, but nothing changed right away. Six months later, though, she forgot to take her medication one night. That was highly unusual for her, but the next morning she felt the Holy Spirit say, "It's time." She felt prompted to stop her medication. Without the usual month-long process of tapering down, she stopped her medicine cold turkey. Going from three pills per night for over 30 years to none would, usually, have been enough on its own to send her body into seizures. But God. This time was different. Elizabeth experienced no withdrawal symptoms and zero seizures. She was completely healed. At the end of her testimony, Elizabeth wrote, "Oh, and I have a new habit. I celebrate Communion every night. I just don't need meds or water to do it now!"

Holy Spirit, thank You for Your sweet presence. I invite Your presence to come even more fully into this moment.

I take Your body, Jesus, declaring that by Your stripes I am healed. You have already paid every price for my healing breakthrough, and I celebrate Your faithfulness.

I take Your blood, knowing that Your blood has cleansed me from everything that is not of You.

If it is not found in Heaven, it will not be found in my life! I declare that I walk in total well-being. I am healed and whole in my body, my soul, and my spirit in the name of Jesus.

Day 15:

OUR DAILY BREAD

Blessed be the Lord—day after day he carries us along. He's our Savior, our God, oh yes! He's God-for-us, he's God-who-saves-us.

—Psalm 68:19 MSG

Jesus, speaking with the disciples, said, "*I am the bread of life; he who comes to Me will not hunger, and he who believes in Me will never thirst*" (John 6:35 NASB95). When Jesus gives the disciples this imagery as a way for them to think about Him, He does something that He does often throughout the Gospels. He is taking a natural reality that they would be very familiar with and using that to explain a Kingdom truth. Our food pyramid has undergone some dramatic shifts recently, but for many cultures bread is a staple food in the normal diet. Jesus had come from the throne room of Heaven. He is the King of all kings. But He doesn't say, "I am the caviar at your dinner party" or "I am the filet mignon of your life," or even "I am like mint chocolate chip ice cream!"

Instead, He says, "*I am the bread of life.*" Bread would have been foundational to the culture at the time. By equating Himself to bread, Jesus relates Himself to something familiar, but not trivial. Bread was intertwined with daily survival. Earlier in that same chapter, Jesus had fed 5,000 from a few loaves and fishes. The disciples had just witnessed the value of bread for the survival of a whole crowd. Bread is life sustaining. Of the 44 nutrients and vitamins necessary for human life found in food, bread made from freshly ground grain has 40.

Unfortunately for all of us, mint chocolate chip ice cream doesn't hold the same nutritional value. When Jesus shares a meal with His disciples on that last Passover, He again offers Himself to His disciples as bread. Jesus breaks the bread, saying, "*this is My body*" (Mark 14:22 NKJV). He offers us the chance to align our bodies with His body, broken and resurrected for us. He is our "*bread of life.*" Our survival depends on Jesus. He is life, hope, and healing.

I never mean to imply that Communion is some sort of golden ticket. Our relationship with God is not transactional; it is relational. Always. But there is power in remembering what He's done for us, of proclaiming who He is to us, and of aligning ourselves—spirit, soul, and body—with His presence. Communion is not just a nice tradition. It represents the body and blood of Jesus Christ. We have access to the transformative power and grace of our Savior. Communion is a powerful tool at our disposal.

We get to come to the Lord with our *choliy*—our grief, our sickness, our pain—and make an exchange. Because of all that Christ did on the cross, we now have access to the same health and wholeness that is found in Him. Our God is the healer. It's not something that He chooses to do or not do; it is who He is. When you take Communion, align yourself with this reality. Plead the blood of Jesus over your soul, your spirit, and your body. And receive His transformative, healing presence into every area of your life.

Jesus, You are the bread of my life. You sustain and nourish me every single day. You are my life, my hope, and my healing.

I hold the bread in my hands—Your body— and I take it, remembering how You were wounded for my transgressions, crushed for my sin.

I take the cup—Your blood—as I proclaim who You are to me. Your blood changed everything.

Today, I once again align myself with Your resurrection power. I declare that my life will reveal Your transformation, grace, and victory to the world.

Day 16:

MAINTAINING PEACE

I leave the gift of peace with you—my peace. Not the kind of fragile peace given by the world, but my perfect peace. Don't yield to fear or be troubled in your hearts—instead, be courageous!

—John 14:27 TPT

On February 21, 2018, my life changed. Earlier that week, I had gone to the doctor for my annual breast thermography, an alternative to the mammogram test. The thermography uses digital infrared imaging to see if there are any "hot spots," an indicator of precancerous cells. The images came back and, while the doctor studied

the results, she became concerned with what she was seeing. Obviously, her concern had me concerned, so just to be sure, I decided to go in for a sonogram as well. When those results came back, the doctor decided to do a needle biopsy on an area of my right breast right there in the office. Then I waited.

Those three days of waiting for the results to come in were torturous. There's nothing like not knowing to leave you feeling powerless and absolutely dependent on God's Word. Deep inside, I felt like I knew what the doctor was going to tell me, but I began to pray and believe that whatever had grown inside of me would disappear.

Three days later, the doctor called me into his office and told me that there was cancer in my right breast. But I was a health advocate! I had written an entire book on health and wholeness called *Healthy and Free*. I had lowered my blood pressure through diet and exercise, and I had lost eight dress sizes in the process. I was careful with everything that I put in and on my body. I'd never felt healthier. So, it all felt like some sort of cruel joke to hear the doctors say the "C" word.

I decided to meet with a top surgeon here in Redding. I wanted a second opinion. She sent me to have more testing done and ultimately agreed with the first doctor. I had cancerous tumors growing in my breast. In addition to the scanning for cancer, I also had my DNA tested. There was a history of breast cancer in my family, so I wanted to see if I had a genetic predisposition for the disease. The test showed an anomaly on one of my genes, basically letting me know that there was a chance that this could reoccur.

After the first doctor's diagnosis, I had already discussed having surgery to remove the two tumors. But when I got the results of the DNA back, I decided to have both breasts removed. Even though it was a more invasive surgery, I knew that having a double mastectomy would help me to maintain my peace in the days to come.

Maintaining my peace has always been important for me, but as soon as I had heard the news, it became essential. Every day after the diagnosis, I was bombarded with new information, medical terminology, and decisions that had to be made as soon as possible. My doctors were wonderful, but every aspect of this circumstance felt like it was attempting to steal my peace. I decided right away, though, that I wouldn't move forward without it.

Jesus, thank You that my level of peace is not dependent on my circumstances. Thank You that peace is not the absence of something—war, chaos, strife—but the presence of Someone. You are the Person of Peace, and today I take communion reconnecting to Your presence.

I take Your body that was sacrificed for me.

I take Your blood that was shed to save me and cleanse me from sin forever.

You are the Lord over my life, and no matter what circumstances I face, I can participate in the perpetual peace of Your presence.

Day 17:

THE PEACE OF HEAVEN

And the peace of God [that peace which reassures the heart, that peace] which transcends all understanding, [that peace which] stands guard over your hearts and your minds in Christ Jesus [is yours].

—Philippians 4:7 AMP

Several years before, a good friend of ours had gone through cancer and beaten it. He wrote a book about his experience called *Kisses from a Good God*. And I began to experience just that. Even on that very first day, when I walked out of the doctor's office with "cancer" ringing in my ears, I felt a kiss from the Lord. As

I walked out that door, feeling scared and overwhelmed, I asked Jesus, "What do I do?" I heard Him say, "Just love Me." A wave of His peace came over me, and I said back to Him, "Okay. I can do that." As I drove home on that first day, I just kept hearing Him say, "You're going to be okay." I clung to that promise.

And so, the journey began. Every day was a choice to walk in peace.

I knew the peace that I was looking for because many years before, I had experienced it in Heaven. Let me explain. I was at a retreat with Judy Franklin. I mentioned earlier that Judy has worked for Bill and me for over 20 years, but she is also highly anointed in taking people on heavenly encounters. She leads people in encounters with the Lord in which they get to experience Heaven with Him. It's a powerful gift.

At this retreat, Judy was speaking, and at the end of her message she had us all lie on the floor, and she began to take us on a journey to Heaven. I was lying on the floor, my head underneath a chair, visualizing Jesus. Almost immediately I went into a vision. In it, I saw my two grandmothers who had passed on. One of my grandmothers was a large, German woman with a powerful, open-mouthed laugh. When I saw her in Heaven, that's exactly what she did. My other grandma had been a wonderful, sweet woman who had taught Sunday school for 25 years. She always had little children around her, and when I saw her in Heaven she looked exactly the same.

It was so special for me to get to see them, but I also realized that I was experiencing something I had never felt before. It took me a while to put my finger on why I felt so different, but suddenly I thought to myself, *Wait, this must be Heaven's peace. I like this.* It's hard to describe, but it was like my mind was quiet for the first time. It was empty of all noise—all of the feelings, worries, and random thoughts that usually are swirling around. It was all gone, and this incredible peace was there instead. As Bill says, once you experience something from Heaven, it's yours forever. I've tried to cultivate that peace—some moments with more success than others—in my life since that moment.

Today and every day I choose to walk in Your presence, God. I choose to lean into Your peace and experience the constant reminders of Your goodness, Your faithfulness, and Your love for me.

I lift up the body of Christ right now, grateful for the reminder that You are in control and You are absolutely trustworthy.

I lift up the blood of Christ, declaring Your kindness over my life and the lives of my family and friends.

Thank You that You have given me Your peace, that which surpasses our understanding, as an inheritance. It is mine forever!

Day 18:

EYES ON JESUS

Therefore, since we are surrounded by such a great cloud of witnesses, let us throw off everything that hinders and the sin that so easily entangles. And let us run with perseverance the race marked out for us, fixing our eyes on Jesus, the pioneer and perfecter of faith. For the joy set before him he endured the cross, scorning its shame, and sat down at the right hand of the throne of God.

—Hebrews 12:1-2 NIV

Taking Communion became one of the kisses from God. I had experienced the power of doing this during Bill's journey back to health, and I grabbed ahold of it during this time. Communion

became an everyday thing for me. I would take the juice and the bread, remembering all that Jesus did for me. I would hold on to the promise of healing given to me through His death and resurrection. And, along with this tradition of taking Communion and applying our healing, there came over me a great peace and assurance.

He was taking care of us, of me. He had already taken care of everything I needed Him to on the cross. I could rest in Him. I knew that if I kept my peace, there would be victory at every turn, in every decision. Whenever I took Communion, and sometimes it was three times a day, it would help me stay focused on Him. His promises would steady my heart.

When I was much younger, I dealt with crippling self-pity. It used to envelop me and drag me down into a deep depression. At 18 years old, I remember crying out to the Lord. I didn't know how to handle the depth of what I was feeling. I knew it wasn't from God, but I didn't know how to live carrying that kind of heaviness. One day, while in the bathroom, I prayed a desperate prayer to God: "If You don't do something to help me, I don't know what's going to happen to me." Instantly, as

I walked out of the bathroom, I was delivered from that spirit. It disappeared and has never returned.

Even though I have been free from self-pity for over 40 years, I dealt with it for so long that I still know what those thoughts feel like. Throughout this health journey, there were times when I could hear self-pity knocking on the doors of my mind. It's a horrible feeling, and I had committed years ago never to fall into it again.

I had to consciously choose not to agree with that spirit and instead focus on the Lord. Communion was an anchor for me. Whenever I was feeling fear or self-pity trying to creep in, my focus had to stay on Jesus. When we take Communion, we are aligning ourselves with God. He suffered in the most extreme ways in order to bring us life and freedom. There's not really room for self-pity when you're focused on that reality.

There is no problem I'm facing today that has surprised You, Father. There is no challenge in my life for which You are not already prepared to offer the perfect solution.

I take Your body, fully dependent on You, my Savior.

I take Your blood, choosing to focus only on You.

You are my anchor in every storm, Lord. You are never caught off guard, overwhelmed, or annoyed by the issues I face. You have come to bring abundance and freedom into every area of my life!

Day 19:

A GOOD FATHER

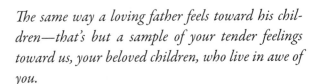

The same way a loving father feels toward his children—that's but a sample of your tender feelings toward us, your beloved children, who live in awe of you.

—Psalm 103:13 TPT

From the very beginning of my health journey, I had decided that I would not have chemotherapy or radiation. My doctors were encouraging me to have both of those things done, but I had no peace about it. So, I knew that that was not the road I would take. When I told my doctors, they said that they understood. They told me that it was my body and that they accepted my decision.

When it came time to choose where I would have the surgery, I already knew what I wanted. I had told Bill many years ago that if I ever needed surgery, I wanted it performed at a surgery facility in our city. This facility was small and quiet, but it had very high ratings for the excellence of their surgery and recovery care. When I went in for the surgery consultation with both of my doctors, they both agreed that the facility I had in mind was a great choice. On top of that, our insurance let me know that my procedure would be covered there.

All of these things may seem small now, but they were huge for me. I'm sure another facility would have done a fine job with my procedure, but that place felt peaceful for me. Each time something worked out like that, it felt like another kiss from God. It reminded me that if something was important to me, it was important to Him. He knew what each of these steps meant to me. He's a good Father. He takes care of His kids, not only in our needs but also in our desires.

In the midst of this, I realized that God had prepared me in many ways for this battle. When the Lord told me, 15 years ago, that He wanted me fit for the long haul, it started me on a journey to health that changed my life. Because of these changes I was strong and healthy—spirit, soul, and body. Soon after I got the diagnosis, I received a word from a friend. He saw the word *benefit* and heard, "Beni is fit for the next season." I did feel extremely healthy, but that fact didn't feel like a cruel joke anymore. It felt like preparation. When I went in to get an EKG before my surgery, the doctor who was looking at my heart said, "Whatever you're doing, keep doing it!" God had prepared me for this fight, and He was going to get me through it.

My first surgery took eight hours to complete. I felt good going into it. I had my friends and family all around me, and I knew they would be in the waiting room the whole time. Because I had decided on proceeding with the double mastectomy, the initial part of the surgery would take five and a half hours. The most crucial part of this step, in my mind, was the biopsy of my lymph nodes. We knew immediately that the tumors in my breast were cancerous, but the doctors wanted to make sure those cancerous cells hadn't traveled anywhere else in my body.

A few weeks before the surgery, I was telling a friend about this who had gone through the same procedure years earlier. She told me that she would pray. A few days later, she called to share what God had told her in a dream. I was to "have *no* concern over the lymph nodes." This was another kiss from God. Obviously, I had been concerned. When the surgeons told me what they were going to do, that reality stayed in my mind, and I had found myself wondering what the results would be. But as soon as she shared her dream with me, that was it. That was all I needed to grab on to that peace. That word sustained me until after the surgery. It was a living word for me. Once I was out of surgery, the surgeons came and gave me the news right away: there was no cancer in my lymph nodes.

Thank You, Father, that You go before me, You stand behind me, and Your presence is all around me.

Jesus, You gave up Your body to be broken on my behalf. I take Your body.

You poured out Your blood as the final sacrifice, so that I would never have to be separated from You again. I take Your blood.

Thank You that, because of what was accomplished on the cross, there is no battle I face that I am not fully equipped to win. You are for me, so nothing can stand against me.

Day 20:

KISSES FROM GOD

Do not yield to fear, for I am always near. Never turn your gaze from me, for I am your faithful God. I will infuse you with my strength and help you in every situation. I will hold you firmly with my victorious right hand.

—Isaiah 41:10 TPT

I experienced another beautiful kiss through God sending me a wonderful, new friend who also happened to be a health coach. She had also overcome stage four cancer through holistic means. Because this was the healing path that I chose as well, I teased her, saying that God had her move to Redding just for me. But seriously, she had experience in just about everything that I was going through. She knew where to send me for advice and what care providers I should see in order to help bring healing on the natural level. She was my constant help in all things holistic, and her encouragement sustained me all along the way. I am forever indebted to her for her constant prayers and instructions.

On her advice, we both ended up going to an amazing holistic clinic in Spain, The Hilu Institute, run by Dr. Raymond Hilu. Honestly, it took me a while to find my peace to go there. I didn't want to leave my family to travel halfway around the world for two weeks. The list of holistic treatments was intimidating, and this was a doctor I didn't know. So I just waited. I knew, by this point, that I wasn't going to do anything without peace, so either I wouldn't go or the peace would come. After a few months, my health coach brought it up again, saying that she would travel with me to Spain. She wanted to undergo another round of treatments for her own care. Soon after, the peace came, and we made the decision to go.

During this entire process, Communion became my frequent morning ritual. It was something that I hung on to through all of the different doctors' reports and decisions that needed to be made. Spending that time with Jesus—recognizing Him and receiving my healing—made all the difference in the world. Some mornings, especially when we were in Spain, I would join with my health coach and we would take Communion together. It was a wonderful time for both of us, committing our lives and our care to Him. I truly believe that this daily alignment was a large part of my healing process.

As I write this, I am walking in health. The doctors' reports continue to be excellent. I will never forget the prayers I received. There were so many people, throughout this journey, who sent me messages, telling me that they were praying and taking Communion for me, people from all over the globe. It's humbling and beautiful to be covered by so many believers. I will always remember this journey, all of my kisses from Heaven, and how Communion continues to play a pivotal role in my health and in my life.

Unity was Your idea, Holy Spirit, and You intentionally bring people around me who will support, challenge, and love me with Your heart.

I take Your body, Jesus, recognizing all that You gave up so that I might join with You for eternity.

I take Your blood, receiving every aspect of Your resurrection power into my life.

I align myself with You. Teach me how You see me. Show me what You think of the people around me. Thank You for the community of believers with whom I can celebrate You, Jesus. Help me to pour out Your lovingkindness on the people around me.

Day 21:

MEDITATING
ON HIM

You will keep him in perfect peace, whose mind is stayed on You, because he trusts in You.

—Isaiah 26:3 NKJV

As soon as I wake up, there are a thousand things competing for my attention. Before my feet hit the ground, I can read news from all over the world, find a recipe for dinner, scroll through photos on Instagram, listen to a worship song, and text my friend. And that's all in a matter of minutes! If the mind is a battlefield, then a big part of the current battle is a fight for space. It's a battle for time, for quiet, and for focus.

Now, I'm not saying that everyone needs to have hours each day set aside for time with the Lord. That's wonderful if you can do that, but not every season of life is conducive to that kind of time. When I was a young mother, that just wasn't possible. I had to learn how to turn my heart toward Him for a few minutes while doing the dishes or putting the baby to bed. What we can all do, though, is to create a meditative space—a space for remembering—during our time of Communion with God.

There are some days that, because of my schedule, I take Communion quickly. But most days I love to take the time to meditate on who God is and what He's done. The Lord wants to reveal different aspects of Himself to us, so every time I take Communion, I ask Him, "What does this mean today? What aspect of You do I need to have at the forefront of my mind today in order to keep myself aligned with You?" He is my daily bread. As I connect with Him, I meditate on His goodness and all that He's done. I take the time to remember.

When Jesus walked the disciples through the first Communion, He commanded them to remember. After both breaking the bread and taking the cup of wine, Jesus says, "*Do this in remembrance of Me*" (1 Cor. 11:24 NKJV). God doesn't need to remember; He lives outside of time. Forgetfulness isn't something He deals with. Remembering is for us. We seem to forget something as soon as we turn around.

Have you read the Old Testament? Part of me wants to shake my head every time I read of the Israelites forgetting the miraculous way God showed up for them two paragraphs prior, but then I think about my own life and how important remembering Him has been for me.

Jesus, I am giving You my undivided attention. You are worthy of my focused love and devotion.

I will quiet my mind as I take Your body, giving myself time to dwell on who You are and what You've done in my life.

I will reject hurry as I take Your blood, asking You to bring to mind an aspect of Your character that is important for me to focus on today.

What does this act of participating in the sacrament of Communion mean for me today? I will wait for Your voice.

Day 22:

REMEMBERING GOD'S FAITHFULNESS

"I will remember the deeds of the Lord; yes, I will remember your miracles of long ago. I will consider all your works and meditate on all your mighty deeds." Your ways, God, are holy. What god is as great as our God? You are the God who performs miracles; you display your power among the peoples.

—Psalm 77:11-14 NIV

Memories have a powerful effect on our attitude and outlook. Bill teaches that if you are having a conflict with a friend, you should only share that conflict with someone who has genuine love for that person. Why? You don't want to vent to someone who will encourage division in the relationship. At that moment, you need someone who is able to remind you—in the midst of the pain—what you love about that person and the value of the relationship. You want someone who can help you pull out of any confusion or defensiveness and into the greater reality of love.

It's similar in weddings. Other than the joy of celebrating with loved ones, we invite our closest friends and family to witness our wedding because, when things get hard, we need those individuals to remind us who we are and what we've promised. Remembrance is vital for our walk as Christians. It keeps us aligned with the reality of who we are and the covenant that was made for us.

I've had many beautiful moments with the Lord throughout my life, but there are a few that I return to more often than others because of how they reorient my heart. One of these moments is our trip to Nome, Alaska. (I have the full details of the story in *The Happy Intercessor.*) I went with a team of women up to northern Alaska to pray over our nation. It was the very first prophetic prayer act that I did out in the community, so I wasn't entirely sure how it was going to work out, but while we were on the trip, it became obvious that every single aspect—where we prayed, what we prayed, the people we met, the timing of our departure—had been orchestrated by God. The time of prayer was powerful, but seeing His attention to detail and feeling so in sync with Him transformed me.

I think back on this moment, and it reminds me not only of His faithfulness but also how alive I feel when I'm connected to the Lord's heart in intercession. It's what I was made to do. I keep those memories close as powerful reminders to myself.

*Father, I thank You for all of the ways
You have shown me Your love and
faithfulness throughout my life.*

*Today, I take the body of Jesus Christ,
remembering Your intentional care
for me throughout my day.*

*I take the blood of Jesus, reminding myself of
all of the ways my true identity
comes alive in You.*

*I will take this moment to dwell on some of
my most influential encounters with You.*

Day 23:

POSSESSING THE PROMISED LAND

I remember the days of old; I meditate on all Your works; I muse on the work of Your hands.

—Psalm 143:5 NKJV

Throughout the Bible, the Lord speaks to His people about the power of memory. In Deuteronomy, the Israelites are about to enter into the Promised Land. They've wandered the desert for 40 years, being sustained and guided supernaturally the whole way. Almost an entire generation has passed away, and the children of those who fled from Egypt are about to walk into the *"land flowing with milk and honey"* (Deut. 11:9 NKJV).

But first, Moses gives them some instructions from the Lord. In the first verse of chapter 11, he repeats the commandment, *"You shall therefore love the Lord your God, and always keep His charge, His statutes, His ordinances, and His commandments"* (Deut. 11:1 NASB95). But then he qualifies this commandment.

Moses says that the people who have seen the miracles of the Lord, the ones who lived through the parting of the Red Sea and the provision of manna, are the ones with the responsibility. *"I am not speaking with your sons who have not known and who have not seen the discipline of the Lord your God—His greatness, His mighty hand and His outstretched arm, and His signs and His works which He did"* (Deut. 11:2-3 NASB95). Moses is charging the ones who have seen the nature of God firsthand with the commandments to love and obey God. The testimony of their lives carries a responsibility, not only for themselves but for the future generations.

He continues, telling the Israelites to remember his words: *"You shall teach them to your sons, talking of them when you sit in your house and when you walk along the road and when you lie down and when you rise up"* (Deut. 11:19 NASB95). "Do not forget who the Lord is, and who He has been to you," Moses says. Why is this so important? I can imagine Moses trying to get through to them, "Guys, please, no more of this idol business. Remember who God is and whose you are. Tell your children. Talk about it all of the time. Use any memory tool that will help you. Write it on your forehead, if that helps!"

He follows this encouragement by explaining to them why this is so important: *"**So that** your days and the days of your sons may be multiplied on the land which the Lord swore to your fathers to give them, as long as the heavens remain above the earth"* (Deut. 11:21 NASB95). Remembering is the key to inhabiting the Promised Land. The Lord wants to pour out blessings on them. He wants to bring them into *"a land of hills and valleys, which drinks water from the rain of heaven"* (Deut. 11:11 NKJV). But in order for them to actually possess this land—to receive this blessing—they need to align their minds with His.

When we take Communion *"in remembrance"* of what Jesus did on the cross, we are stewarding the greatest testimony in history. The Israelites escaped Egypt after ten supernatural plagues rained down on their captors. They walked through the Red Sea on dry land. They were led by pillars of cloud and fire. They were fed supernaturally, never got sick, and wore the same clothes for 40 years. Yet they didn't have Jesus. They didn't have the cross or the resurrection. They didn't have a Savior who took away the sins of the world. Matthew 11:11 makes it clear the kind of gift we have received. *"Truly I say to you, among those born of women there has not arisen anyone greater than John the Baptist! Yet the one who is least in the kingdom of heaven is greater than he"* (NASB). John the Baptist knew Jesus as family, followed God faithfully, yet he was never born again. He didn't know life with the resurrected Christ living inside of him. You and I, we get that honor. We have that responsibility.

You long to pour out blessings upon my life, Lord, and I am forever humbled and grateful for that. In order to step into the land of promise that You have in store for me, I will treasure the testimonies of Your supernatural intervention.

I take the body of Your Son, remembering all of the ways Your love has changed my life.

I take the blood of Your Son, recalling the testimonies throughout Scripture that are now my inheritance.

I will not take all that was accomplished at the cross for granted.

Day 24:

DO IT AGAIN, GOD

Finally, believers, whatever is true, whatever is honorable and worthy of respect, whatever is right and confirmed by God's word, whatever is pure and wholesome, whatever is lovely and brings peace, whatever is admirable and of good repute; if there is any excellence, if there is anything worthy of praise, think continually on these things [center your mind on them, and implant them in your heart].

—Philippians 4:8 AMP

Memory is a powerful tool. It shapes our present by creating expectation for repetition. The brain is literally creating pathways from your thought patterns. Some of the discussion of this began in the New Age movement, but now scientists who study the brain are confirming what the Bible says—what you allow your mind to dwell on shapes your expectations and, ultimately, your perception of the world. The neurons in the brain strengthen and change with our thought patterns. The more you make certain connections, the more likely your brain will make that connection in the future. Some describe it similarly to the way a popular hiking trail gets worn down and widened. For example, if you're used to thinking the world is out to get you, that neuropathway will have a strong connection in your brain. Something might happen to you, and you think, "Well, there it goes again. I knew bad things happen to me."

But the grace of the Lord always makes room for transformation. You can change these neuropathways by what you set your mind on. So, when Paul writes to the Colossians and advises them, "*Set your mind on the things above, not on the things that are on earth. For you have died and your life is hidden with Christ in God*" (Col. 3:2-3 NASB95), it's not just a nice idea. It's actually advice that will change the "hardwiring" of our brains. We are new creations. We know a reality that is greater than any circumstance we can see. We have "*the mind of Christ,*" and God is inviting us to use it (see 1 Cor. 2:16).

Bill spoke about the power of testimonies recently. At Bethel, sharing testimonies is a big part of our culture. We have a two-hour senior staff meeting each week where we spend 90 percent of the time sharing about what the Lord is doing all over the earth. It's amazing to hear about the miracles. The world is truly getting better all of the time. But when we hear those, we don't just stop with marveling at God's goodness. We also say, "Do it again, God!" As Bill says, the power of the testimony never depreciates.

Whenever you revisit a story of God's faithfulness or His divine disruption in your life, you are revisiting a place of divine encounter. Remembering what He's done in your life never loses power. God is the same yesterday, today, and tomorrow. So when you hear of a miracle that has happened in someone else's life, you know that God has just set the legal precedent of what He wants to continue. Testimonies are not just fond memories. They have a life span that's eternal. They continually give God praise.

A beautiful thread weaves between our past, our present, and our future. In our past, we have what God has done—all of the stories of His faithfulness and grace. In our present, we have the command to remember those testimonies, to build our trust in God and align ourselves with Him. From that place, change will come. *"For whenever you eat this bread and drink this cup, you proclaim the Lord's death until he comes"* (1 Cor. 11:26 NIV). The act of proclaiming is like sharing the testimony. It is releasing the reality of the cross into the world.

When you're remembering God and trusting in Him completely, then you are filled with hope for the future of the world around you. We can take Communion in remembrance of all that He has done for the world and for ourselves personally, and we can look toward the future with hope. Matthew 17:20 says, *"If you have faith the size of a mustard seed, you will say to this mountain, 'Move from here to there,' and it will move; and nothing will be impossible for you"* (NASB). This promise is embedded in the body and blood of Christ.

I will not allow the size of a problem to overshadow the size of You, God. Your power, Your love, and Your redemption are at the very core of my reality.

If ever I forget, I will take Your body, proclaiming the testimony of Jesus' death and resurrection.

If ever I get distracted by circumstances, I will take Your blood, returning once more to my experiential knowledge that You are absolutely trustworthy.

Because of who You are, I look out at the world with hope above every concern. I anticipate Your goodness in every situation. I trust You no matter what.

Day 25:

HE GAVE THANKS

As for me, may I never boast about anything except the cross of our Lord Jesus Christ. Because of that cross, my interest in this world has been crucified, and the world's interest in me has also died.

—Galatians 6:14 NLT

Often, we don't really want to remember the brutality of what Jesus went through for us. It's gruesome and uncomfortable. But when I remind myself of the details of Christ's death, I find that it keeps my heart in a posture of overwhelming gratitude. It also renews my perspective on whatever challenge I'm going through. For 33 years, Jesus had lived on earth, three of those spent serving in a fruitful, but probably exhausting, time of public ministry. As He neared the end of His life, Jesus wrestled with what He was about to do.

He knelt down and prayed, saying, "Father, if it is your will, take this cup away from me; nevertheless not My will, but Yours, be done." Then an angel appeared to Him from Heaven, strengthening Him. And being in agony, He prayed more earnestly. Then His sweat became like great drops of blood falling down to the ground" (Luke 22:41-44 NKJV).

Jesus was the only one, besides the Father, who was aware of what He was about to go through. The intensity of that anticipation, not only of His own physical death but also of the agony of being separated from the Father because of the sin of the world, must have been so painful that He literally sweat blood. When He was carrying that reality, the betrayal by Judas and the rejection from His closest disciples must have been an added weight on His heart.

When I take Communion, I stop and remember this betrayal. I don't just dwell on the injustice for its own sake, but I do want to remember the cost of what Jesus did so that I can truly value His gift to me. Thinking through all that He went through in the days leading up to His death also paints a picture to me of how to walk through pain. These moments in the life of Jesus are so brutal and yet so beautiful.

Jesus knew that Peter would deny Him, that His disciples would abandon Him, and that Judas was going to betray Him. But He still sat down to a meal with them and shared Communion. "*The Lord Jesus, on the night he was betrayed, took bread, and when he had given thanks, he broke it*" (1 Cor. 11:23-24 NIV). There are a few aspects here that teach me so much. He was well aware of the betrayal, yet Jesus still invited Judas to break bread with Him. He gave thanks. Jesus filled His heart with gratitude, despite being aware that He was about to die and the very people He was dying for were betraying Him. I can't imagine the strength that Jesus had to have to walk through that moment the way that He did. Knowing that He was going to be crucified, He gave thanks. In the midst of betrayal, He opened His heart to His disciples.

Jesus, I lift up the pain my heart is experiencing right now. I know that You know what grief, disappointment, and anger feel like.

I take Your body, giving thanks for who You are to me.

I take Your blood, offering up a sacrifice of praise in the midst of my own pain.

You are worthy of it all, Lord. You suffered in every way imaginable—physical torture, heartbreaking betrayal, and agonizing separation from the Father—all because of Your incredible love for me.

Day 26:

THE BETRAYAL OF JESUS

And by the blood of his cross, everything in heaven and earth is brought back to himself—back to its original intent, restored to innocence again!

—Colossians 1:20 TPT

When I'm remembering the betrayal of Jesus, I'm not just focusing on the injustice. I'm focusing on Jesus. I'm reminding myself of the way He walked through betrayal. If Jesus can do that, then He's offering me a model for how to deal with my own hurts and grievances. He's showing me what His love can overcome.

I remember the day that this point really hit home for me. I was taking Communion with my husband. Over the years, we have experienced a few people who have focused a lot of energy on attacking our lives and ministry. That day, when we were in the middle of praying for our friends and family, Bill started to pray for each of the people who had come against us. He began to pray a blessing over their families, praying for God's grace to be on their lives and for their physical health. I sat there, listening to my husband, and felt totally convicted. I remembered what Jesus went through, and something clicked in my spirit. I realized, "Oh my gosh, I can love these people. Despite everything that's going on, I can love them."

Jesus didn't shy away from the suffering involved in His sacrifice. The agony of anticipation He experienced in the Garden of Gethsemane and the betrayal by Jesus' disciples was followed by excruciating physical pain. He was forced to carry a heavy cross for miles while a crowd threw stones at Him and spit in His face. Once the cross was erected, long nails pierced through the tendons in His wrists and the bones in His feet. For three hours, our Jesus suffered the most horrifying pain as He hung on the cross, experiencing the weight of sin and the distance of the Father.

As a part of meditative Communion, I like to remind myself of what He went through on the cross. One day, I was imagining His suffering, and I realized, "He stayed up on that cross!" Jesus was fully God and fully man. He didn't have to do anything He didn't want to do. He could have taken Himself right off of that cross if He'd chosen to, but He stayed. He stayed for me. He stayed for us. That realization brought a whole new wave of gratitude, because I know that I couldn't have done that. I would have been saying, "Sorry, Dad, but I can't handle this!" Instead, He stayed.

There is a weight to remembering the cost that Jesus paid. I never want anyone to cultivate the heaviness that leads to depression. But there is an important humility and gravity that comes when you are remembering *how* His body was broken for us and *how* His blood was poured out for us. When I meditate on His experience, I remember all over again that His blood is sufficient for anything I am going through. Jesus paid the ultimate sacrifice so that I could be free and whole. If something is threatening that, I know it's not of the Lord. I can see what He went through to untangle me forever from sin and sickness.

Jesus, You were wounded for my sins, crushed for my wickedness, and punished so that I could live life in peace, fully healed and restored to the Father.

I take Your body, lifting up in prayer people who have betrayed me or caused me pain. Would You pour out Your blessings on them and their family?

I take Your blood, releasing forgiveness and peace over each one of those painful situations in my life. I will choose—like Jesus—to answer pain with love, betrayal with blessing, disappointment with worship.

Day 27:

DWELLING ON HIS GOODNESS

We will not conceal them from their children, but tell to the generation to come the praises of the Lord, and His strength and His wondrous works that He has done. For He established a testimony in Jacob and appointed a law in Israel, which He commanded our fathers that they should teach them to their children, that the generation to come might know, even the children yet to be born, that they may arise and tell them to their children, that they should put their confidence in God and not forget the works of God, but keep His commandments, and not be like their fathers, a stubborn and rebellious generation, a

generation that did not prepare its heart and whose
spirit was not faithful to God.

—Psalm 78:4-8 NASB95

Dwelling on the goodness of God, continually reminding ourselves of His faithfulness and His promises—these are the building blocks of trust. And, when we trust God, aligning ourselves with His commandments comes so much more naturally. Without our keeping Him in the forefront of our minds, that confidence crumbles, and fear takes hold.

I love how *The Passion Translation* puts it in verse 22 of Psalm 78, talking about the Israelites who forgot God: "*They turned away from faith and walked away in fear; they failed to trust in his power to help them when he was near.*" There are very real consequences to our forgetting who God is. When His goodness and faithfulness are not fresh in our mind, we can become calloused toward God. We can feel hesitant to trust in His goodness. And that can lead to a heart that has not been cultivating gratitude.

We can see the results of that within our own lives and the lives of the Israelites. As soon as they started forgetting, they began to fear, and they put their trust in something else. Later, the same psalm speaks of the Lord's reaction to their unfaithfulness. *"He abandoned the dwelling place at Shiloh...and He gave up His strength to captivity and His glory into the hand of the enemy"* (Ps. 78:60-61 NASB). This verse is incredibly sobering. Because of the Israelites' forgetfulness, because they turned from trusting in God completely, He allowed His presence to be removed from their midst. They were no longer recipients of His strength, and they no longer had access to His glory.

We live under the New Covenant. God has promised never to remove His presence from us, but we still have the same choice that the Israelites had. Will we remember and trust in God's love for us, or will we turn to fear and fending for ourselves? The psalmist describes an all-too-familiar heart issue: *"Even when they saw God's marvels, they refused to believe God could care for them"* (Ps. 78:32 TPT). Will He take care of me? Will He provide for me? Was His blood enough for what I'm going through? Each time we take Communion, we are testifying to the enormous, radical love of God. We are reminding ourselves that we had a debt that we could never, ever repay and that we were condemned to death; there was nothing we could do about it.

But God. His love was so extravagant that He sent His Son to die in our place, to suffer indescribable pain so that He could take on the sins of the world. *"For God so loved the world, that He gave His only begotten Son, that whoever believes in Him shall not perish, but have eternal life"* (John 3:16 NASB95). This was the first verse I learned as a child. It's a powerful one that we can take for granted because it's so familiar. I would encourage you, as you take Communion, to meditate on this verse. Allow your remembrance of Him to take you to a new level of understanding. It was all for love. Love took Him to that cross, and love kept Him there. When you take Communion, experience the invitation to remember the weighty reality of His absolute and perfect love for you.

*Your love was so deep, so all-encompassing,
God, that You sacrificed Your greatest
treasure—Your Son—so that sin and death
no longer had a hold on me. You valued me
so much that You paid an incomprehensible
price to restore our connection for eternity.*

*I take the body of Your only begotten Son,
pierced and broken for my sake.*

*I take the blood of the One in whom You were
well pleased, spilled out so that I might live
in freedom with You.*

*I will never forget Your sacrifice; I will
never doubt Your goodness in my life.*

Day 28:

HEALING
THE LAND

*If My people who are called by My name will humble
themselves, and pray and seek My face, and turn from
their wicked ways, then I will hear from heaven, and
will forgive their sin and heal their land.*

—2 Chronicles 7:14 NKJV

In 2016, I felt like the Lord asked me to take Communion every day for the 15 days leading up to the presidential elections. So every day at high noon, I would take my little cup and wafer and remember all that Jesus did for us and all that He was doing in our nation. High noon has become an important time for me to pray.

When the sun is at its pinnacle in the sky, everything is exposed. I like to think about the light flushing out anything that's been hiding in the dark places. It's a powerful time to intercede for God's light and truth to expose any hidden things.

I was born to pray. When I go up to the high places—a mountaintop or the top of a city building—to pray and worship, I feel as though I'm doing what I was born to do. I'm in my element. I often go with a team of friends to various places to intercede, and in the last few years we've added Communion to the arsenal of tools we use during these times.

Too often Communion can get locked into the routine of church culture. There are great, logistical reasons for churches to have Communion once per month. But that doesn't mean we have to limit ourselves to that! Like every other aspect of our walk with God, if we are only experiencing Communion within the four walls of the church, we are missing out on a gift from Jesus.

Communion is a powerful tool of intercession. And because of that, it's applicable in every area of our lives. At the end of 2017, Bethel invited people to prayer walk in their neighborhoods for three months. In that time, people traveled alone or with friends to whatever part of the city they had on their hearts. We offered a list of prayer targets, but those walking were encouraged to pray, take Communion, and declare truth over our city and our nation. One of the ways that we can tap into the transformative power of Communion is by taking it into our communities. These walks are a chance for us to take ownership over our land and the atmospheres over our cities.

Anne Kalvestrand, a powerful intercessor at Bethel, shared an example of this kind of geographical ownership. In 2015, students who had gone through our Bethel School of Supernatural Ministry traveled on a ministry trip to Turkey for the 100-year anniversary of the Armenian Holocaust. This genocide was the horrific killing of around 1.5 million Armenians after World War I, which displaced many surviving Armenians from their land. The alumni who were on this trip were all either of Armenian or Turkish descent. Together, they traveled to the location of some of the conflicts, and they poured the Communion elements onto the ground, praying for the trauma of the genocide to leave the land. The Armenian students forgave the Turks and prayed for salvation to come to all of Turkey.

Holy Spirit, thank You for the ways that You are moving throughout the land. Thank You that You know exactly how we can pray effectively for every geographic area.

I take Your body, Jesus, declaring that Your work on the cross is finished.

I take Your blood, announcing that the grave is empty, the stone was rolled away, and that You rose in absolute victory over all forms of death and destruction.

I am now able to participate in Your victorious resurrection, releasing the authority of Heaven onto the earth and taking ownership over the atmosphere surrounding me.

Day 29:

PROCLAIMING THE GOSPEL

And it's true: "Everyone who calls on the name of the Lord Yahweh will be rescued and experience new life." But how can people call on him for help if they've not yet believed? And how can they believe in one they've not yet heard of? And how can they hear the message of life if there is no one there to proclaim it?

—Romans 10:13-14 TPT

First Corinthians 11 says that, when we participate in Communion, we are proclaiming the Lord's death. *"For as often as you eat this bread and drink this cup, you proclaim the Lord's death till He comes"*

(1 Cor. 11:26 NKJV). On the surface, that verse sounds like we're just reminding everyone that Jesus died. But it's more than that. That phrase *"you proclaim"* is the Greek word *kataggello*. It's the same word, used throughout the New Testament, that is also translated as *preached*. *"And when they arrived in Salamis, they **preached** the word of God in the synagogues of the Jews"* (Acts 13:5 NKJV).

When you take Communion, you're telling the world about the Lord's death. Every time you partake in the body and blood of Jesus Christ, you are preaching the Gospel. How? Communion is most often thought of as a time of quiet reflection, not bold proclamation. Yet that word *kataggello* is undeniably assertive.

Each time you take Communion, you align yourself with the broken body and the shed blood of Christ. You are remembering what He's done for you. But you are also aligning yourself with what happened three days later.

When those Turkish and Armenian students stood together and poured out Communion onto the war-ravaged soil, they were inviting the reality of the resurrected Christ, the One who is victorious over sin and darkness, into the history of that land. When we are lined up with the reality of Christ—in spirit, soul, and body—we release that reality into the world.

We preach the Good News, not just from a pulpit or with our voices; we preach the Good News with who we are. We show the goodness of God with how we handle situations in our businesses and in our families. Every time we take Communion, then, we are reminding ourselves that we are Christians—little Christs. When we remind ourselves who we are, we can reveal to the world who He is.

*Jesus, I want every aspect of who I am
to speak loudly to the world of Your
goodness and Your faithfulness.*

*You are the God of restoration; there is
nothing that Your presence cannot heal. So,
I take Your body that was broken for me,
declaring restoration into every
broken area of my city.*

*You are the resurrected Christ, so I plead
Your blood over my community.
I take Your blood, proclaiming
Your victory over darkness.*

*My city will be saved, healed, and
delivered in the name of Jesus!*

Day 30:

RELEASING THE KINGDOM

God be gracious to us and bless us, and cause His face to shine upon us—Selah. That Your way may be known on the earth, Your salvation among all nations.

—Psalm 67:1-2 NASB

When we remember who He is and who we are, we can offer the world a glimpse of a God they may have never seen before. We can reveal to them a Father who cares, who desires to be intricately involved in every aspect of their lives. Andy Mason, the head of Heaven in Business, has been teaching this principle to people in the business sector for years. For too long, people who have been called by God to ventures outside of the church have received the message that their jobs were somehow less spiritual. But by teaching businessmen and women about how much God longs to be a part of their companies, Andy has started to see incredible miracles of provision, new ideas, and healing inside of businesses.

He has been using Communion in his ministry to the business world as well. He has taken Communion into the prisons. There, the inmates are taught on Communion as a tool for healing, and they then take Communion with whatever food and drink the prisons provide for them. Andy explains to the inmates that they don't have to have someone lay hands on them to be healed. God is healing, so when He is present, healings happen. Andy has seen countless miracles within the prisons. We never want to reduce Communion to something small. No matter what we are using to take Communion, the importance is remembering the fullness of what Jesus paid for and receiving that fullness into every area. And, as Andy says, "If it can happen in your body, it can happen in your business."

He told the story of one international business friend who had started to press in to see more of God in his business. He'd already had a string of miraculous encounters with God's provision. With these testimonies behind him, he launched a new business with two different sides to the company. One side was getting a lot of traction and growing, but the other side had not started to move. Andy joined his friend in praying for breakthrough, thanking God for the miracles they had already witnessed in this man's life. Andy explained, "I felt like we should take Communion, pray, and bless the business, believing that Jesus had already paid for everything within his business."

They took Communion inside of the office, and Andy was dropped off at the train station to catch his flight back to the US. By the time Andy was walking through customs back in the States, he had received an email from his friend. As soon as he had dropped Andy off, the man had returned to work. Once he arrived, though, he discovered that the once-stagnant workplace had suddenly received at least ten requests for quotes from all over the world from huge international companies. They were in business! The owner was so blown away by the presence of the Lord that he couldn't work for the rest of the day.

The Lord wants to invade every area of your life. He is not only interested in being with you in Heaven; He wants Heaven to invade earth in your families, in your businesses, and in your communities. The Bible says that He knows *the very hairs of your head* (Luke 12:7 NKJV). He knows what is in our hearts, and He cares about what we care about.

Thank You, Father, that I can come boldly before Your throne because of what was accomplished at the cross. I know that I have a Savior who intercedes on my behalf. There is no area of my life in which I have been left alone to figure things out.

I take the body of Jesus Christ, knowing that I have access to every type of breakthrough.

I take Your blood, Jesus, declaring that there is no area of my life in which You are not intimately invested.

Father, I invite You to invade my family, my friendships, my health, my career, my dreams, my city, and my country. Show me Your heart for every part of my life!

Day 31:

NO JUNIOR
HOLY SPIRIT

*Jesus said, "Let the little children come to me, and do
not hinder them, for the kingdom of heaven belongs
to such as these."*

—Matthew 19:14 NIV

Some people grow up feeling terrified of Communion. Not so much because of the "*eat my flesh and
drink my blood*" part (see John 6:56), but more
often because of what it says in First Corinthians 11:27,
"*Therefore whoever eats the bread or drinks the cup of the
Lord in an unworthy way, shall be guilty of the body and
the blood of the Lord*" (NASB). I was talking to a friend

recently who said that when she was young, she would frantically search her memory for every sin she could have committed in the last month. She would confess anything and everything, thinking that if she missed something, she might die right there on the wooden pew. Every month held a renewed sense of terror as she reached for the bread and juice.

This is not how it's supposed to be. It's funny to talk about now that she's an adult, but experiencing the sacrament of Communion is not something that should terrify our children. Communion is a powerful way to encounter the Lord, and we get to invite them into that with expectation. Seth Dahl, co-author of *Win+Win Parenting*, led Bethel's Children's Ministry for seven years. He does a brilliant job of empowering children to have their own God encounters.

Children do not have a junior Holy Spirit. On the contrary, they often have an easier time connecting with the presence of the Lord because they don't have years of "stuff" to unlearn. When leaders come into our environment needing a prophetic word, we will often ask the kids to minister to them. Their purity, fearlessness, and lack of religion seem to allow them to hear God's voice in a way that often leaves their audiences profoundly moved.

But God wants to use them to change the world just as much as He wants to use an adult. They have access to Him in the same way, and Communion can be a powerful tool for them to connect with the presence of God. But often, it feels a bit intimidating to try to teach kids about something like Communion. Seth broke down how he does it, explaining that the most important things to focus on when teaching children anything are to wipe out fear, make it fun, and take our time.

Seth uses Hebrews to help give the kids a visualization of the New Covenant as he introduces Communion:

Therefore, brethren, since we have confidence to enter the holy place by the blood of Jesus, by a new and living way which He inaugurated for us through the veil, that is, His flesh, and since we have a great priest over the house of God, let us draw near with a sincere heart in full assurance of faith, having our hearts sprinkled clean from an evil conscience and our

bodies washed with pure water (Hebrews 10:19-22 NASB95).

The juice represents the blood of Jesus, he explains to the kids, and this blood gives us access into a place we were never able to go before. Before Jesus died, only a few very special people could go in to the presence of God. No one else could. So, when we drink the juice, we're remembering that we can go *boldly* before the presence of God. It's not just the high priest who can enter the presence of God—all of us can!

Seth explains to the kids about the veil that was torn. The veil is like His flesh, so when we take Communion, we are saying, "Thank you, Jesus, that You have torn the veil and that You've washed us in Your blood so that we can come into the presence of God." He encourages the kids to remember what Jesus gave us on the cross, remember what He did—our old, sinful man has passed away, His blood washed us as white as snow, and we are raised again as a new creation. We are now saints! We also remember that by His stripes we are healed. So we're not just remembering the moment Jesus died on the cross; we're remembering all that the cross did for us.

Thank You, God, that You have made Yourself so accessible to me. It is not hard to reach You; I do not have to strive. I will never be found unworthy of Your love. I come to the gift of Communion, today, like a child.

I take Your body, surrendering all to Your perfect will.

I take Your blood, joyfully celebrating that I can approach Your presence boldly, without fear or insecurity.

My heart has been made clean by Your sacrifice, and I run into Your arms, experiencing Your delight in me.

Day 32:

RELEASE
THE KINGDOM

*I will give you the keys of the kingdom of heaven; and
whatever you bind on earth shall have been bound in
heaven, and whatever you loose on earth shall have
been loosed in heaven.*

—Matthew 16:19 NASB

Many years ago, we had a strange experience
where a roadrunner kept coming to our
prayer meetings. For months, this bird would
show up outside of the building when we would gather
to worship. We had no idea what was going on, but it felt
significant. One night, the bird snuck into the building

while one member of our custodial team was cleaning. Every time the custodian would stop working to put on some worship music, the bird would stop and watch. Every time the young man would move, the bird would follow him.

After a while of this, a door opened from another room and spooked the bird. It ran down the hallway into the plate-glass window and died. The whole story was too strange, so Bill went to the Lord and just asked Him what was going on with this bird. Very clearly, he heard, "What I'm bringing into the House had better have a way of being released from the House or it will die in the House."

The Spirit of God lives inside every believer and will never leave. But we have the honor of stewarding His presence. God has given the gift of His body and blood to His Church. But I want to encourage you to release the power of Communion from the four walls of the church and into your family, your business, your community, etc. There is no area of your life that Communion with God cannot improve.

The Bible says that *"the testimony of Jesus is the spirit of prophecy"* (Rev. 19:10 NKJV). Whatever God has done before, He wants to do again. Grab hold of every testimony. Let your faith rise. Align yourself with the resurrected Christ. And witness the wonder-working power of Jesus.

Holy Spirit, thank You that You know the exact ways to speak to me so that I can hear You. Thank You that You live within me for my sake, but that You come upon me for the sake of the world.

I participate in the broken body of Jesus, standing on the truth that His sacrifice was made for every single person.

I take His blood, releasing the reality that the resurrection power of Heaven is available through Him.

Every area of my life glistens with hope because of what Jesus has done for me on the cross. Nothing is impossible with You, God!

Day 33:

PARTICIPATING WITH REVERENCE

Therefore, since we are receiving a kingdom that cannot be shaken, let us be thankful, and so worship God acceptably with reverence and awe, for our "God is a consuming fire."

—Hebrews 12:28-29 NIV

Jesus never requires perfection in order to come to Him. That is the scandal of His saving grace. We don't need to be anxious about taking Communion, searching for any potential hidden sin. Fear is never productive; it just gets in the way of love's transforming power. However, when we participate in the body and blood of Christ, we do want to posture our hearts in an intentional way. This intentionality not only brings the respect and honor due to the sacrament, but it also helps us to create the space in our hearts for the Spirit of God to move and transform us through Communion.

Often, when we focus so much on what divides us, we can miss out on honoring some valuable aspects of different Christian traditions. Even though I love our free-flowing worship, there is something so beautiful about a formal liturgy. Similarly, I think we can learn from the way the Catholic Church honors Communion, teaching the children what it means and making a special event of their first occasion. When we participate in Communion, it is important for there to be a sense of soberness. I don't mean *somber*, as in "gloomy or depressing." Far from it.

But there needs to be a sense of gravity about what we are getting to participate in. Our sobriety points to the very real power of Communion, a time when we get to remember the gravity of what has been done for us on the cross. We get to participate in the blood and body of

Christ with as much reverence and honor as that reality demands.

We have such a good Father, who is so incredibly full of grace, but I would never want to lose sight of His holiness or His awesome power. On the one hand, we have Jesus, inviting the little children to come to Him. And on the other, we have Jesus, returning to earth with eyes that flame like fire. It's not either/or; it's both/and. When we participate in the body and blood of Jesus Christ, sober reverence is a healthy and appropriate reaction.

*You are holy, Lord, and You are worthy of
every offering of praise I could ever lay at
Your feet. I come before You in reverence, in
awe of who You are and of Your power that
moves on the face of the earth.*

*I take Your body, Jesus, aware of the gravity
of what it cost You to invite me
into eternal life.*

*I take Your blood, worshiping
You with a purely devoted heart.*

*You are a consuming fire and
I stand amazed by You.*

Day 34:

PARTICIPATING WITH THANKFULNESS

It's so enjoyable to come before you with uncontain-
able praises spilling from our hearts! How we love to
sing our praises over and over to you, to the matchless
God, high and exalted over all! At each and every
sunrise we will be thanking you for your kindness and
your love. As the sun sets and all through the night,
we will keep proclaiming, "You are so faithful!"

—Psalm 92:1-2 TPT

Thankfulness is showing appreciation. The Bible
tells us to "*Rejoice always; pray without ceasing; in*
everything give thanks; for this is God's will for you

in Christ Jesus" (1 Thess. 5:16-18 NASB95). I often hear people yearning to know God's will for their lives, but it says it right here. Stay thankful. Stay connected to God.

When the Bible tells us to be thankful no matter the circumstance, it is not expecting us to create an emotion out of thin air. Gratitude is a response. There has to be a previous action or reality. When we take Communion, we are responding to all that the Lord has done and continues to do for us. Keeping our hearts postured toward the Lord in gratitude is one of the biggest keys to success we find throughout the Bible.

Hebrews 13:15 encourages us to "*continually offer up a sacrifice of praise to God*" (NASB). We've all been in the midst of experiences where the phrase "*sacrifice of praise*" feels very real. When you're exhausted or hurting, sometimes worship and expressing gratitude is the last thing you want to do. But look at the Samaritan leper. Ten leprous men were healed by Jesus, but only one of them fell down to give Him thanks. Jesus wasn't in need of gratitude, but He knew that it would do something for the man.

Jesus asked about the other nine men who hadn't returned, and then He told the Samaritan, "*Stand up and go; your faith has made you well*" (Luke 17:19 NASB). The man was already healed. But that word "*well*" is that Hebrew word *sozo* again. His body had been healed, but there was something about his expression of gratitude that made him whole.

Psalm 50 says that "*He who offers a sacrifice of thanksgiving honors Me; and to him who orders his way aright I shall show the salvation of God*" (Ps. 50:23 NASB95). This is such a powerful verse. We have been made "*a royal priesthood*" (1 Pet. 2:9 NASB). As believers under the New Covenant, we now have the privilege of ministering to the Lord. When we offer up a "*sacrifice of praise*," we are bringing honor to God.

Focusing our hearts on gratitude brings Him glory, which alone is enough. But the Bible goes on to explain that gratitude also reorients us correctly, inviting the "*salvation of God*" into our lives. That word *salvation* is the Hebrew word *yesha*, which means "rescue and safety," but it also means "deliverance, prosperity, and victory." The psalmist said to "*enter His gates with thanksgiving and His courts with praise*" (Ps. 100:4 NASB95). When we come to the Lord with thankfulness, we have access to His presence and His covering. We get to participate in His victory.

I have so much to be thankful for, God. Even in my most challenging seasons, my gratitude for You cannot be contained. Even if there are things in my life that are trying to distract me from having a thankful heart, I will choose to give thanks in all things.

I take Your body, overwhelmingly grateful for every sacrifice You made for me.

I take Your blood with thankfulness overflowing in my heart for Your presence, for Your blessings, for Your healing in my life, and for Your never-ending love for me.

I will rejoice always in You!

Day 35:

PARTICIPATING WITH CELEBRATION

Finally, beloved friends, be cheerful! Repair whatever is broken among you, as your hearts are being knit together in perfect unity. Live continually in peace, and God, the source of love and peace, will mingle with you.

—2 Corinthians 13:11 TPT

I love the story of the first miracle that Jesus did. I love that Mary pulled Jesus' public ministry into the limelight before it was time. And I love that Jesus created wine for a party. Jesus loves celebration. The dictionary defines *celebration* as "the action of marking one's pleasure at an important event or occasion by engaging in enjoyable, typically social, activity."

We can celebrate alone, of course, but more often a celebration is an experience we want to share with the people we love. When we take Communion, it is our chance to celebrate with our brothers and sisters in Christ. Jesus has changed our lives, and that deserves a party. After all, what's a celebration without friends? We may focus mostly on taking Communion individually, or maybe family members taking it together. But there is something very special about corporate Communion—partaking of the body and blood of Christ with the vibrant, diverse Body of Christ. Communion is a vertical realigning of ourselves with Christ, but it is also a horizontal realigning—we are the Body of Christ.

God loves unity. It was His idea. This is why examining our hearts is such an important part of Communion. Not because we have to prove to God that we're worthy of His blood and body. We already know that's impossible. We examine our hearts because it's a time of reunion, both with the Spirit of God and with our fellow believers. In corporate Communion, we get to stand with others and confess that He took a burden from our shoulders that we could never carry. Experiencing that radical grace means that we now get to access and release that grace to others. We get to offer forgiveness to others, cleansing our hearts from the detrimental effects of bitterness and unforgiveness.

The individual relationship with God is crucial to our lives and foundational to our beliefs. We must have that time in the secret place. But the Lord also loves it when we gather, united, in His name. He promises that "*where two or three have gathered together in My name, I am there in their midst*" (Matt. 18:20 NASB).

Communion is a time of celebration. Like eating the wedding cake and toasting with champagne after the vows have been exchanged, Communion commemorates the covenant that has been made between our Creator and ourselves. This celebration also solidifies and reminds us of the union that we have with those around us. Jesus loves His Church. He is coming back for a strong, healthy, and united Bride.

You deserve to be celebrated every moment of every day, Jesus! You have changed my life completely. You have grafted me into Your family of believers. I get to call myself a child of God because of all that You've done for me. That alone deserves a party!

I take Your body, today, acknowledging that I am one part of Your Body on the earth. I stand with my brothers and sisters in Christ, rejoicing over who You are and what You have done.

I take Your blood, confessing that I have received a grace that I could never have earned. Because of Your blood, I have been empowered to release that grace onto others.

I will preserve the unity that began with You, God.

Day 36:

ALIGNING OURSELVES WITH HIM

And we all, with unveiled face, continually seeing as in a mirror the glory of the Lord, are progressively being transformed into His image from [one degree of] glory to [even more] glory, which comes from the Lord, [who is] the Spirit.

—2 Corinthians 3:18 AMP

It's all about Him. Everything changes when we align ourselves with God. As Bill says, "The Holy Spirit wants to reveal Himself *to* you so that He can reveal

Himself *through* you." We are citizens of Heaven, but we have an assignment to fulfill on earth—that is releasing the reality of Heaven into every situation, every relationship, and every corner of the earth.

But how can we do that? Not through our own strength, surely. Scripture says that *"we have the mind of Christ"* (1 Cor. 2:16 NKJV). It says that we have died and have been raised with Jesus (see Rom. 6:4). It says that our old man has gone and we are a new creation (see 2 Cor. 5:17) and that Christ lives within us (see Gal. 2:20). The Bible is 100 percent true, so if I'm not experiencing those statements all of the time, then there must be a reality that is greater and *truer* than the one that I am experiencing.

That we would need reminding of this greater reality comes as no surprise to the Lord. It's like He sat us all down at that table with the disciples in that upper room and said, "Listen, I know. I know some days are going to be hard. I know there are going to be moments when it feels like the reality of Heaven is far away. Your child is sick or you lost your job or your best friend died or you did that thing you swore you would stop doing. I know.

I'm leaving you something—My body and My blood—to remind you who you are and where your true home is. I'm leaving you this reminder of My salvation, My healing, the comfort of My presence, and My victorious return. Take it. Remember Me. Be everything I created you to be so that My Kingdom can invade every single one of those situations, and the world can know a good, good Father."

Human nature is constantly attempting to create rules outside of a relationship. Communion is not a magic pill, and God is not a vending machine. He does not want us to eat a wafer and drink some grape juice every day so that He will grant our wishes. Communion is about lining ourselves up with Him—spirit, soul, and body. It is a chance for us to remember the debt of sin that hung around our necks—too big for us to ever repay on our own—and the way that our Jesus took that debt with Him to the cross so that you and I could *have life, and have it abundantly*" (John 10:10 NASB). It's a chance for us to come—in all humility and honor—into the presence of the Lord, to praise His name for all that He has done, and to celebrate in union with other believers. Take this tool, given to us by Jesus Himself, and use it frequently. You will not remain the same. That is His promise.

I come to You today, God, exactly as I am. I take all of my questions, fears, and doubts, and I lay them at Your feet. You have given me the sacrament of Communion as a reminder of Your goodness, Your faithfulness, and the cost You paid for our connection.

I take Your body, Jesus, remembering that I was set free from the crushing debt of sin.

I take Your blood, declaring my new reality: I have the mind of Christ. I am a new creation, Jesus Christ lives within me!

Day 37:

BOASTING IN GOD

My old self has been crucified with Christ. It is no longer I who live, but Christ lives in me. So I live in this earthly body by trusting in the Son of God, who loved me and gave himself for me.

—Galatians 2:20 NLT

We are taught in the Scriptures that in taking Communion we are *proclaiming the Lord's death until He comes* (see 1 Cor. 11:26). I like to picture *proclaiming* as a bold and confident shout! We are declaring in fullness the redemptive work of Jesus found in the Gospel. Every time we take the bread and the wine/juice in remembrance, it is a prophetic proclamation of what has already happened, as well as what is yet to come. Consider this—Communion declares that Jesus died for us and is returning for His us.

When people surrender their life to Jesus, they are born again. In other words, they're saved. We know this teaching from God's Word. But then the Bible also says, *"Work out your own salvation with fear and trembling"* (Phil. 2:12 NKJV). The implication is that I am also *being saved*. This doesn't deny what happened to me when I received Christ. It just emphasizes the daily ongoing process of personal transformation. So, not only were you once saved, but you are also being saved right now.

The crowning touch to this glorious truth of our salvation comes when we die to meet Him or He returns to take us to Heaven. In this coming event, we find that we *will be* saved. Our salvation will then be complete. Participating in Communion is a wonderful privilege that declares what I call *the bookends of our salvation* in that it addresses the past and the future. Sharing in the broken body and the shed blood of Jesus helps us with the present.

The most complete passage on the rite of Communion in the Bible is found in First Corinthians 11. In it, Paul unwraps the insight given to him through an encounter with Jesus Himself. In verses 23 and 24, he says, *"For I received from the Lord that which I also delivered to you: that the Lord Jesus on the same night in which He was betrayed took bread; and when He had given thanks, He broke it and said, 'Take, eat'"* (NKJV).

Please picture something powerful—the very night that Jesus was betrayed, He gave thanks. In the midst of the ultimate betrayal, He gave an offering of thanksgiving. He didn't just tell us to praise Him in hard times; He gave us the ultimate example to follow. In betrayal, He gave thanks.

Following the major sporting events like the Super Bowl, World Series, World Cup, and the like, it has become common to see athletes thank God for enabling them to win. I love to see them boast in God and testify of Him every chance they get. But let's be honest, it's not that challenging to give thanks when you've won. The real prize is when we give Him thanks in the middle of something difficult or wrong. That's where the pearl is formed, so to speak. Pearls are formed through irritation. Whenever we give thanks in the middle of hard things, we are presenting something to Him that is priceless. Jesus did it at His darkest moment—betrayal.

You are exactly who You say You are, God. Everything You have done in the past prophesies to my future. You died for me, and You are returning for me.

I take Your body, participating in the reality that Your death on the cross saved me, I am being transformed daily into Your image, and I will unite with You in Heaven.

I take Your blood that was shed for me, giving You thanks in the midst of every hardship I am experiencing right now.

You are worth all of my praise! No matter what circumstance I am in, I will worship You and give You thanks.

Day 38:

PARTAKING IN A WORTHY MANNER

For you know that your lives were ransomed once and for all from the empty and futile way of life handed down from generation to generation. It was not a ransom payment of silver and gold, which eventually perishes, but the precious blood of Christ—who like a spotless, unblemished lamb was sacrificed for us.

—1 Peter 1:18-19 TPT

Paul gives us a somber warning: *"Whoever eats the bread or drinks the cup of the Lord in an unworthy manner, shall be guilty of the body and the blood of the Lord"* (1 Cor. 11:27 NASB95). This is an interesting part of Communion. Communion hurts you if you're not saved but advances you if you are. The anointing of God doesn't always have the same effect on people. The presence that brings you peace will sometimes irritate others.

Paul admonishes, "*Let a man examine himself, and so let him eat of the bread and drink of the cup*" (1 Cor. 11:28 NKJV). Verse 29 is key for us. "*For he who eats and drinks in an unworthy manner eats and drinks judgment to himself, not discerning the Lord's body*" (NKJV). Paul is defining what it looks like to eat and to drink in an unworthy manner. None of us are clean enough on our own to be worthy to participate in Communion. Jesus is the One whose blood makes us clean enough to celebrate the broken body and blood of Jesus. It is His provision for us. But in this context, Paul is explaining that judgment has come through a lack of discerning the body.

When Jesus broke the bread, He said, "*This is My body*" (1 Cor. 11:24 NKJV). And Paul said people eat judgment to themselves by not discerning the body correctly. Every time you take Communion and are holding the bread in your hand, you hold something that has value, deserves recognition, and can carry judgment. When we hold the bread of Communion, we recognize that it is a divine moment.

The body in this context is most likely referring to the bread we hold in our hands. But there is also reason to think He is referring to the Body of Christ, which is the people of God. Both perspectives have merit and are easy to apply in this setting. Placing correct value on the bread I hold, believing it is the body of Jesus, has tremendous impact on the effect of that act. But it could also be said that giving proper esteem to the people of God as the Body of Christ also has value in this context. The point is, don't reduce this to a mindless ritual. Think, pray, and give thanks.

Paul goes on to say, "*That is why many of you are weak and ill, and some have died*" (1 Cor. 11:30 ESV). He is saying there are people in the Body of Christ who will go to Heaven, but because they did not realize the meaning of what was in their hands, they reduced Communion to a religious ritual. Without realizing it, they removed the tool that God had put in their life to bring divine health. And for that reason, many are weak or sick, and some have even died. Yet presumably, week after week, month after month, the miracle was in their hand. But a wrong perspective cancels out the power of that moment. One book calls this "the meal that heals." Well said.

Father, I am so grateful for the precious, holy gift that You have given us in Communion.

I take the body of Your Son, acknowledging that it was Jesus' sacrifice that washed me clean. I could never have done that on my own.

I take the body as a priceless, sacred gift.

I take the blood of Jesus, that which cleansed me from all unrighteousness and set me free. Your blood covers me, Jesus, so that I might participate in Your worthiness and experience Your miraculous power in my life. I receive everything You paid for on the cross.

Day 39:

ON EARTH AS IT IS IN HEAVEN

Our Father in heaven, hallowed be your name, your kingdom come, your will be done, on earth as it is in heaven.

—Matthew 6:9-10 NIV

Isaiah 53, the prophetic passage on healing, reads, *"Surely He has borne our griefs"* (verse 4). The literal word for *griefs* is *sicknesses*. In this passage, Isaiah is, in fact, saying, "Surely He has borne our sicknesses. He carried our pains. Yet we esteemed him stricken, smitten by God and afflicted." When Jesus died on the cross, the Scripture says, "He became sin" (see 2 Cor. 5:21). And when He became sin and died in our place, the Father's anger and wrath were poured out on Him as He became the very thing that was working to destroy us.

He took my place and bore what I deserved. Jesus asked the Father, "Why did You turn Your face from me? Why did You forsake me?" (See Matthew 27:46 and Psalm 22:1.) The Father forsook Him because Jesus became sin. He poured out His wrath upon His own Son, who had become what was destroying mankind.

When we say that *"by His stripes we are healed,"* we're talking about the beating that He endured. We're talking about the moment when Jesus made a payment for our health and our healing. This part of His suffering was not to make it possible for us to go to Heaven. This one, in many ways, is for Heaven to come to earth in us. His blood paid the price to get you to Heaven. But His stripes were actually a payment for our pain, suffering, and sicknesses here on earth.

Everybody knows you get a new body in Heaven. There's no sickness there; there's no weeping there; there's no pain, no conflict, no confusion. In Heaven, everything is wonderful. So it's important to see that this part of His provision is for now. *"By His stripes we are healed"* (Isa. 53:5 NKJV). Peter quoted the passage from Isaiah in this way: *"by whose stripes you were healed"* (1 Pet. 2:24 NKJV). Notice it is past tense. It has already been accomplished on our behalf.

The body of the broken Savior made a full and complete payment, not only for my healing but for health—spirit, soul, and body. This is the provision of the Lord. And that's its purpose. Remembering Jesus' broken body in Communion is not just a nice sentimental moment when we give thanks that He died and we get to go to Heaven. It is all that, but a million times more. It's a divine moment.

I will forever by humbled by Your mercy, Jesus. You bore all of the pain and punishment that I deserved so that I might experience all of the peace, healing, and love of Your Kingdom.

I take Your body, the body You offered up as my replacement, suffering physically under the weight of my sin. It is by Your stripes that I have been healed.

I take Your blood, declaring that Your blood covers me, releasing divine health into my spirit, soul, and body so that I might experience the reality of Heaven released on earth.

Day 40:

IMPACTING
THE NATIONS

For behold, the darkness shall cover the earth, and deep darkness the people; but the Lord will arise over you, and His glory will be seen upon you. The Gentiles shall come to your light, and kings to the brightness of your rising.

—Isaiah 60:2-3 NKJV

I try to take Communion every day. While I'm not always successful, Beni and I have made this a regular part of our daily life, even when traveling. When we do this in our corporate gatherings, it looks a bit different in that it takes a few minutes of our service. But when

I'm alone, or with Beni, we like to take a bit more time than is reasonable in our corporate Communion time on a Sunday morning.

Beni and I often take Communion together, but a couple of years ago I got too sick to even take Communion. Beni would sit by my bed and take it for me. We would just sit there together and give thanks to God for His goodness. She would take Communion, we'd hold hands, and we'd pray. We would just thank the Lord for His provision, for healing, for divine health. Our approach to life is to see in completion what Christ had accomplished for us and make the decree, "By His stripes I was healed" (see 1 Pet. 2:24).

It's important to remind ourselves as we take Communion that it is because of the sacrifice of the Lamb of God that we are alive, that we are forgiven, that we have hope. I pray this reality over each individual in my family.

The promise of household salvation carries over into the New Testament. The jailer was saved, and soon after his encounter his entire household was converted (see Acts 16:31-34). That is the standard of the Lord. Don't settle for any other. Don't be impressed with the sin your loved one may be involved in; be impressed with the power of the blood of Jesus.

I believe in the power of Communion so much that I love to make confession over my family of how the blood of Jesus sets us free. This confession absolutely terrifies parts of darkness. I know from personal experience that it's the one thing of which they are absolutely terrified. They know that the blood of Jesus is the dividing line that separates someone the demonic can control from someone they can't touch.

I love to hold this before the Lord and pray for the people around me. I just plead the blood of Jesus over their lives. I want to encourage you to pick up a similar habit. It's not just grape juice that we're drinking. I pray that each of us would fully realize the effect of what we're doing during Communion. I believe that the Lord is going to release unusual miracles of healing in the taking of the bread. He is going to release unusual miracles of deliverance to people and family members who are maybe a thousand miles away or more by our taking the juice (representing the blood) and pleading the blood of Jesus over their lives.

Prayer while partaking of Communion is possibly one of the most underrated prayers that we could ever pray. Communion is not a magic formula. It's us being convinced that the blood of Jesus sets free. And that expression of faith puts us into a position to influence the destinies of our families, the people around us, and the entire world.

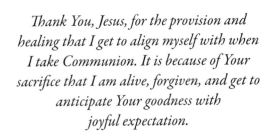

Thank You, Jesus, for the provision and healing that I get to align myself with when I take Communion. It is because of Your sacrifice that I am alive, forgiven, and get to anticipate Your goodness with joyful expectation.

I take Your body, declaring healing and health over every member of my family. Sickness, pain, and sorrow no longer have any authority over my life or the lives of the people I love.

I take Your blood, confessing the fact that Your blood has set each person free. There is no one who is out of Your reach. I will name out loud the people I know who are far from You, God, as I plead the blood of Jesus over their lives.

You have paid the price for my freedom, deliverance, and healing. Your miraculous power is going to invade my life and the lives of those around me. Thank You, Jesus, that I am aligned with You to influence my family, my community, and the entire world for Your Kingdom. Let Your will be done on the earth!

ABOUT THE
AUTHOR

Beni and her husband, Bill Johnson, are the senior pastors of Bethel Church. Beni has a call to intercession that is an integral part of the Bethel Church mission. She was pivotal in the development of Bethel's Prayer House as well as the intercession team. Beni also carries a call to see the church become healthy and whole in their bodies, souls, and spirits. Her heart is to see the people of God live lives that are healthy and free and see them pave the way to bringing health back to the world as God intended. Her passion for people, health, and intercession have all helped to bring the much-needed breakthrough in Bethel's ministry. Beni's vision is to see the people of God live lives filled with joyful prayer, intercession, and complete wellness.

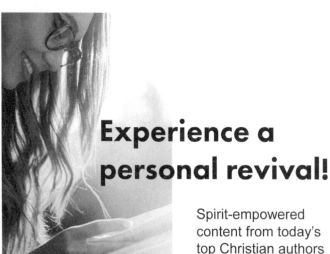